SUMMER JOURNAL

HOW TO USE THIS JOURNAL.....

This journal includes :

- A page to record your thoughts at the beginning of summer.
- A page for bucket-list activities and a blank bucket list page to add your own items to the list.
- Pages to record the books that you read during the summer.
- Daily log pages to talk about the things that happened on the day.
- Pages with some summer-related questions, activities that you can fill out in any order.
- Few blank pages to add anything that you don't find an appropriate place for in the book.

There is no right or wrong way to fill this journal. This is your journal so feel free to do it in your way. Use stickers/draw/write/stick photos...Use whatever you want to capture your memories. However, here are some tips to help you!

- Set aside 5-10 minutes daily and fill out the daily log page. Flip through the questions/prompts to see which one you really want to do that day. Questions/prompts at the beginning of the journal are more related to the beginning of the summer and ones towards the end are more related to the end of the summer. But remember, order is not important.
- During the day, if you are doing something that you might want to enter in your journal, take a picture, or collect something etc.
- Feel free to scratch some questions out, write new ones of your own.

Summer is the best time of the year and we all do so much during summer without even realising. This journal is a fun way for you to look back, on things that you have done, experiences you have had and memories you have made. This will be an awesome keepsake for you to see how wonderful the summer was!

MY ADVENTURES OF SUMMER

ME :

I am _____ years old.

My favorite thing about summer is

My goal for this summer is

One thing I want to learn this summer

MY SUMMER BUCKET LIST

- ☐ Have a water-balloon fight.
- ☐ Make/Eat popsicles.
- ☐ Go to a museum.
- ☐ Visit the zoo.
- ☐ Create a lemonade stand.
- ☐ Tie-dye a t-shirt/towel/anything else.
- ☐ Go to a beach.
- ☐ Paint kindness rocks and put them around.
- ☐ Do some cool sidewalk chalk pictures.
- ☐ Picnic in the park.
- ☐ Make s'mores.
- ☐ Go berry-picking.
- ☐ Go to the pool.
- ☐ Run through sprinklers.
- ☐ Fly kites.
- ☐ Visit Farmer's market.
- ☐ Watch fireworks.
- ☐ Bury a time capsule.

MY SUMMER BUCKET LIST

- [ ]
- [ ]
- [ ]
- [ ]
- [ ]
- [ ]
- [ ]
- [ ]
- [ ]
- [ ]
- [ ]
- [ ]
- [ ]
- [ ]
- [ ]
- [ ]
- [ ]
- [ ]

BOOKS I READ

- [ ]
- [ ]
- [ ]
- [ ]
- [ ]
- [ ]
- [ ]
- [ ]
- [ ]
- [ ]
- [ ]
- [ ]
- [ ]
- [ ]

BOOKS I READ

- [ ]
- [ ]
- [ ]
- [ ]
- [ ]
- [ ]
- [ ]
- [ ]
- [ ]
- [ ]
- [ ]
- [ ]
- [ ]
- [ ]

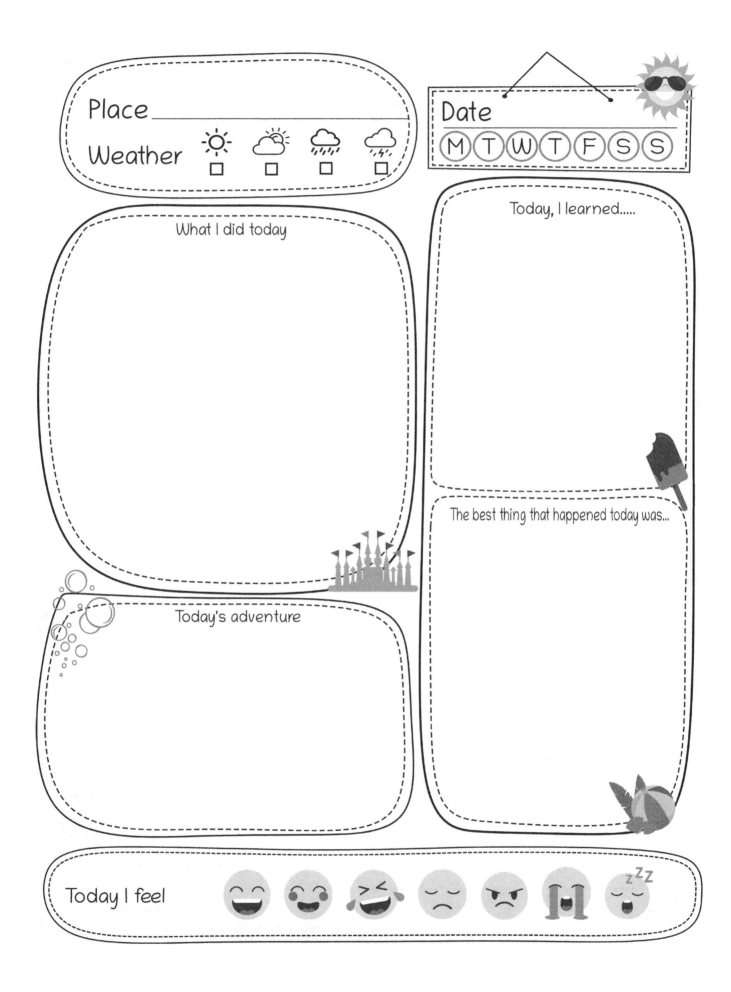

Place _____

Weather ☀ ⛅ 🌧 ⛈
☐ ☐ ☐ ☐

Date _____
Ⓜ Ⓣ Ⓦ Ⓣ Ⓕ Ⓢ Ⓢ

What I did today

Today, I learned.....

The best thing that happened today was...

Today's adventure

Today I feel

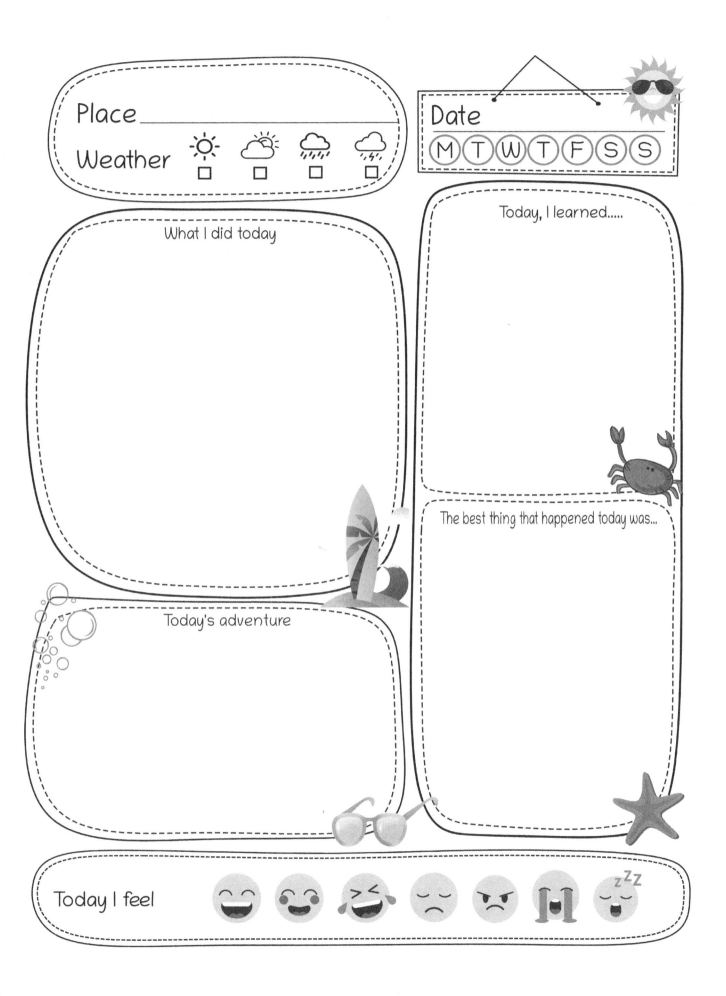

Place _____

Weather ☀ ⛅ 🌧 ⛈
□ □ □ □

Date _____
Ⓜ Ⓣ Ⓦ Ⓣ Ⓕ Ⓢ Ⓢ

What I did today

Today, I learned.....

The best thing that happened today was...

Today's adventure

Today I feel

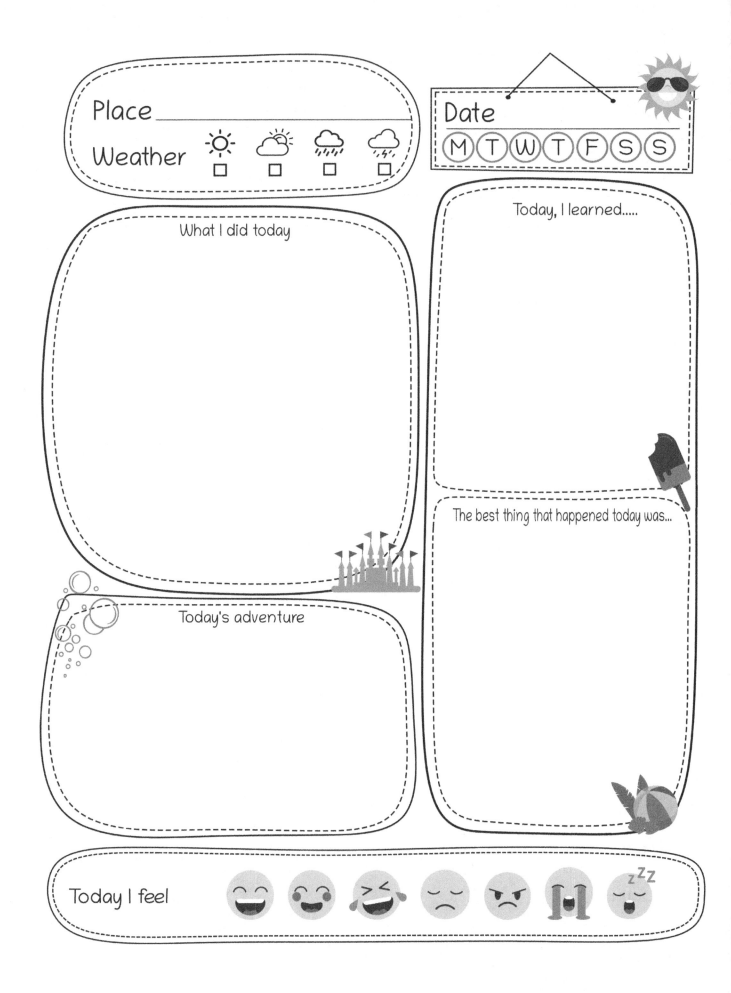

Place _____

Weather ☀ ⛅ 🌧 ⛈

Date _____
M T W T F S S

What I did today

Today, I learned.....

The best thing that happened today was...

Today's adventure

Today I feel

Place _____

Weather ☀ ⛅ 🌧 🌧
□ □ □ □

Date _____
Ⓜ Ⓣ Ⓦ Ⓣ Ⓕ Ⓢ Ⓢ

What I did today

Today, I learned.....

The best thing that happened today was...

Today's adventure

Today I feel

My favorite memory from last summer is...

The thing I am looking forward to most this summer is

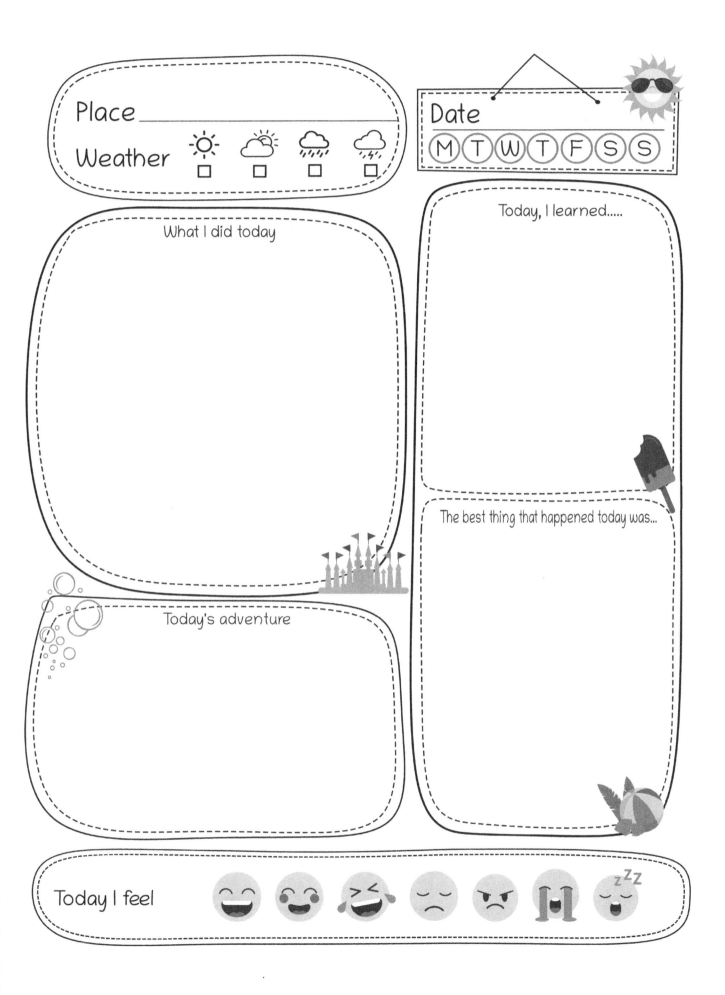

Place _____

Weather ☀ ⛅ 🌧 ⛈

Date _____
M T W T F S S

What I did today

Today, I learned.....

The best thing that happened today was...

Today's adventure

Today I feel

Place _____

Weather ☀ ⛅ 🌧 ⛈
         ☐ ☐ ☐ ☐

Date _____
M T W T F S S

What I did today

Today, I learned.....

The best thing that happened today was...

Today's adventure

Today I feel 😄 😊 😆 😔 😠 😭 😴

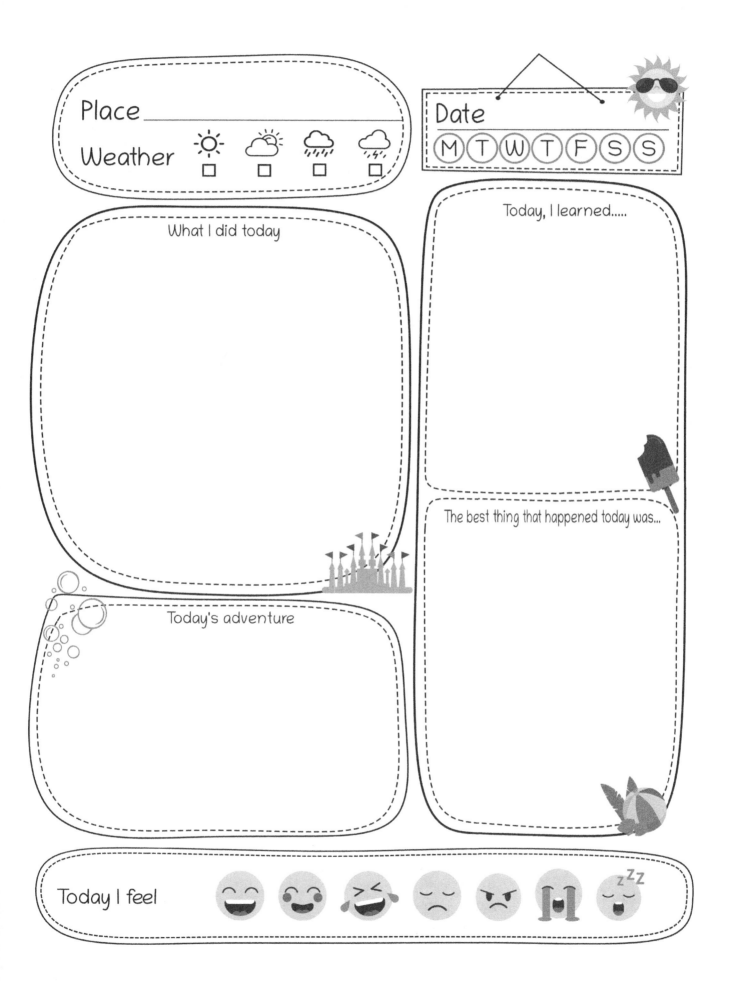

Place _____

Weather ☀ ⛅ 🌧 ⛈

Date _____
M T W T F S S

What I did today

Today, I learned.....

Today's adventure

The best thing that happened today was...

Today I feel

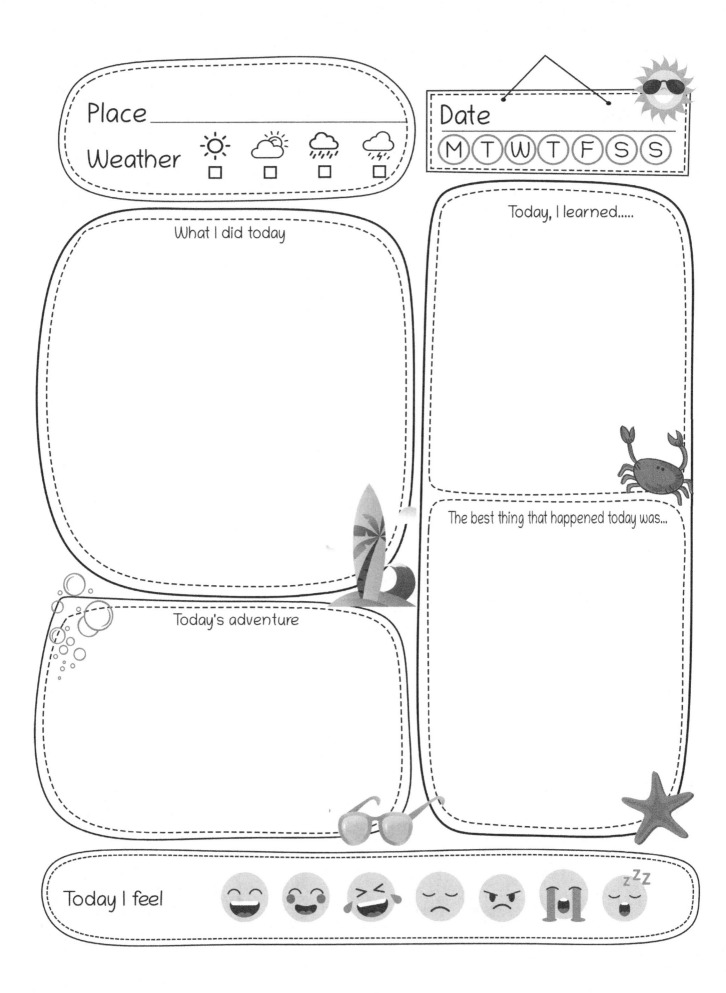

Place _____

Weather ☀ ⛅ 🌧 ⛈
☐ ☐ ☐ ☐

Date _____
Ⓜ Ⓣ Ⓦ Ⓣ Ⓕ Ⓢ Ⓢ

What I did today

Today, I learned.....

The best thing that happened today was...

Today's adventure

Today I feel   😄 😆 😂 😔 😠 😭 😴

My ideal summer day would go like this......

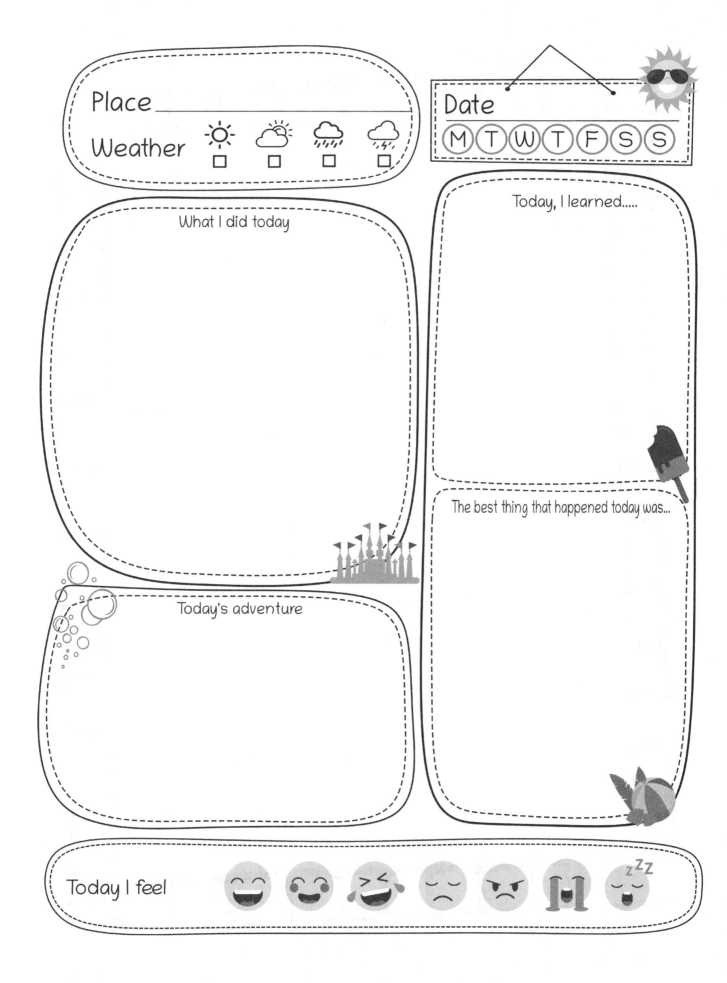

Place _____

Weather

Date

M T W T F S S

What I did today

Today, I learned.....

The best thing that happened today was...

Today's adventure

Today I feel

Place _____

Weather ☀ ⛅ 🌧 ⛈

Date _____

M T W T F S S

What I did today

Today, I learned.....

The best thing that happened today was...

Today's adventure

Today I feel

Place _____

Weather ☀ ⛅ 🌧 ⛈
□ □ □ □

Date _____
Ⓜ Ⓣ Ⓦ Ⓣ Ⓕ Ⓢ Ⓢ

What I did today

Today, I learned.....

The best thing that happened today was...

Today's adventure

Today I feel

If I could have a super-power this summer, this is what it would be.

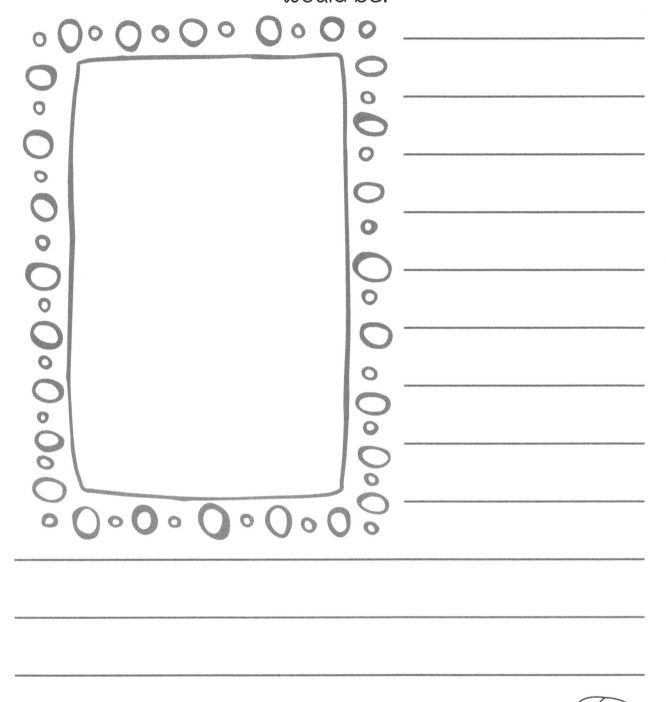

_____

_____

_____

_____

_____

_____

_____

_____

_____

_____

_____

_____

_____

_____

Can you draw your super-hero avatar and describe what you would do?

Place _____

Weather ☀ ☁ 🌧 ⛈
□ □ □ □

Date _____
Ⓜ Ⓣ Ⓦ Ⓣ Ⓕ Ⓢ Ⓢ

What I did today

Today, I learned.....

The best thing that happened today was...

Today's adventure

Today I feel 😄 😊 😆 😞 😠 😭 😴

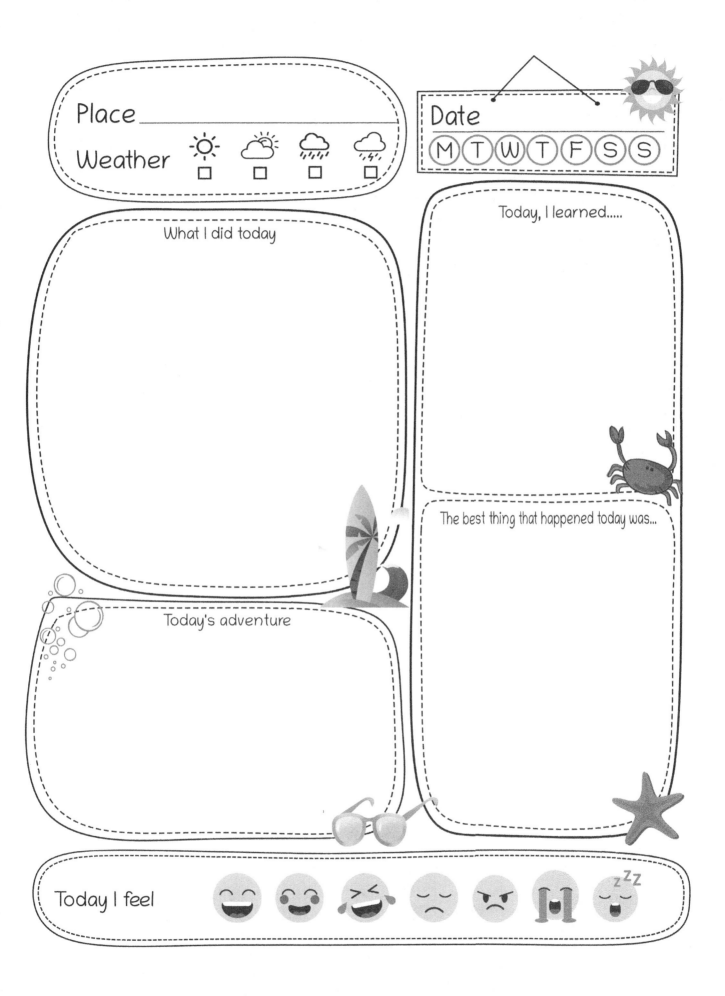

Place _____

Weather ☀ ⛅ 🌧 ⛈

Date _____
M T W T F S S

What I did today

Today, I learned.....

The best thing that happened today was...

Today's adventure

Today I feel 😄 😊 😆 😔 😠 😭 😴

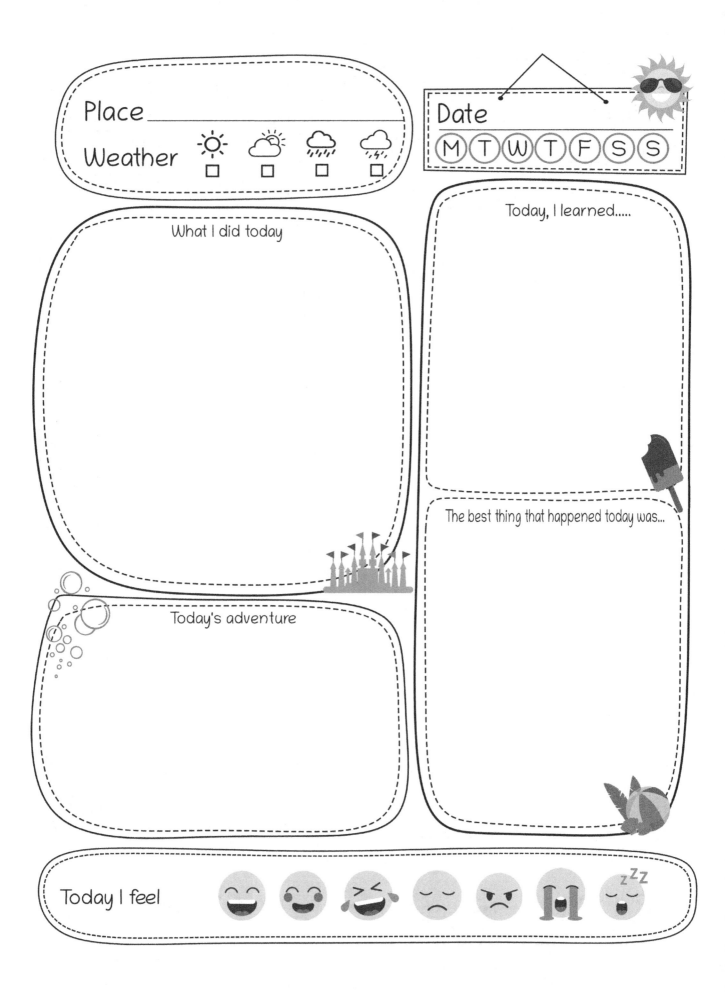

Place _____

Weather ☀ ☁ 🌧 ⛈
□ □ □ □

Date _____
M T W T F S S

What I did today

Today, I learned.....

The best thing that happened today was...

Today's adventure

Today I feel   😄 😊 😆 😞 😠 😭 😴

My favorite food is....

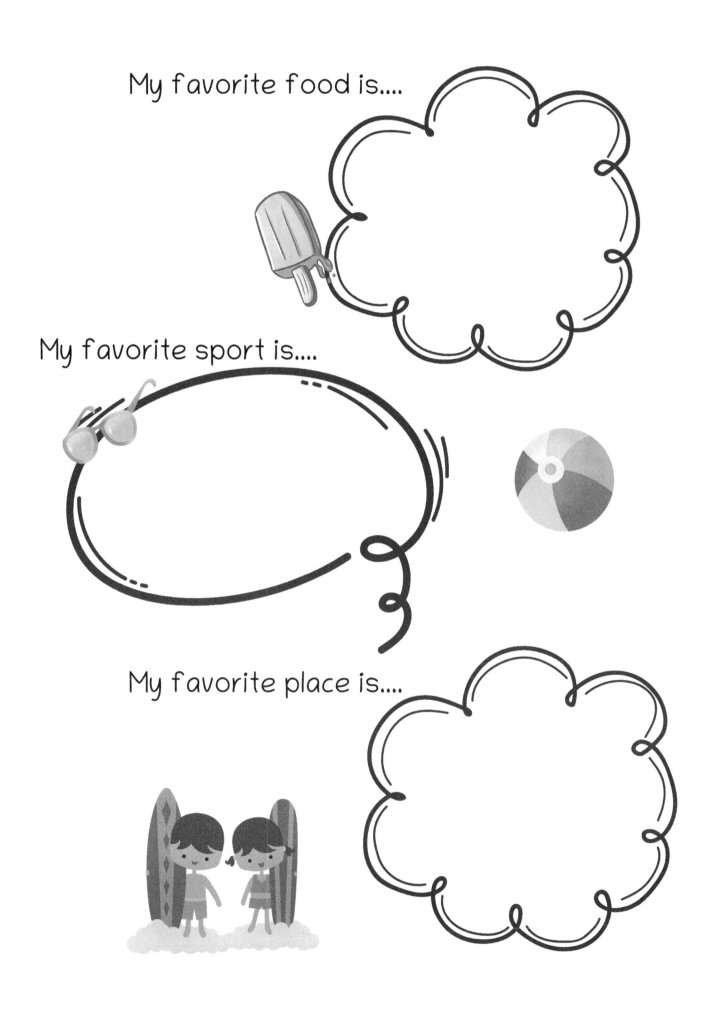

My favorite sport is....

My favorite place is....

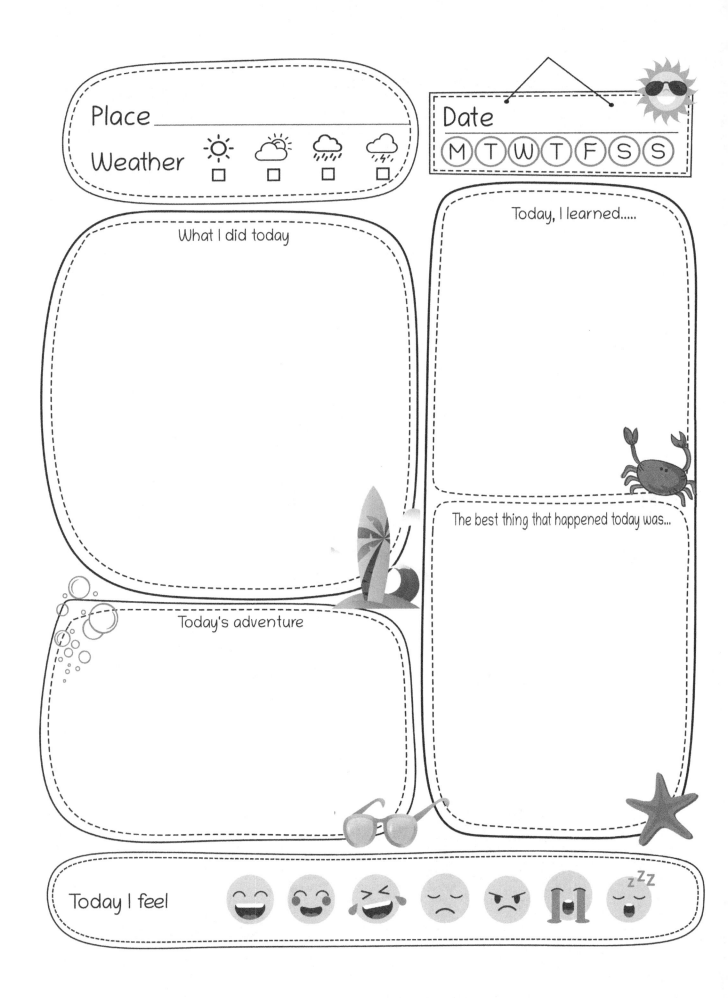

Place _____

Weather ☀ ⛅ 🌧 ☁
☐ ☐ ☐ ☐

Date _____
Ⓜ Ⓣ Ⓦ Ⓣ Ⓕ Ⓢ Ⓢ

What I did today

Today, I learned.....

The best thing that happened today was...

Today's adventure

Today I feel

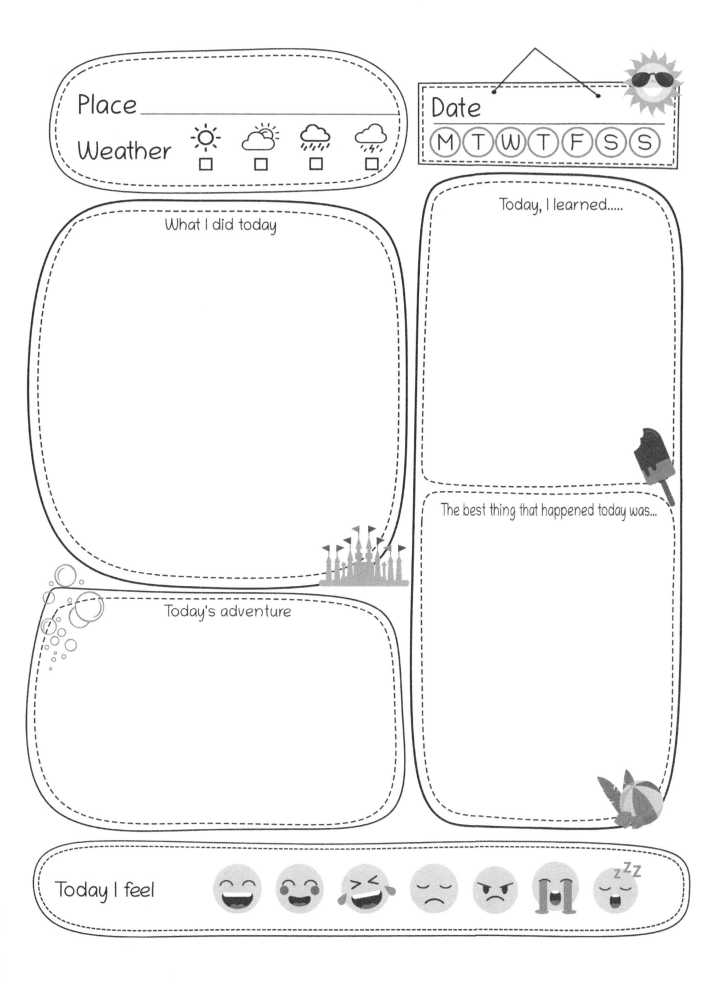

Place _____

Weather ☀ ⛅ 🌧 ⛈
         ☐ ☐ ☐ ☐

Date _____
M T W T F S S

What I did today

Today, I learned......

The best thing that happened today was...

Today's adventure

Today I feel

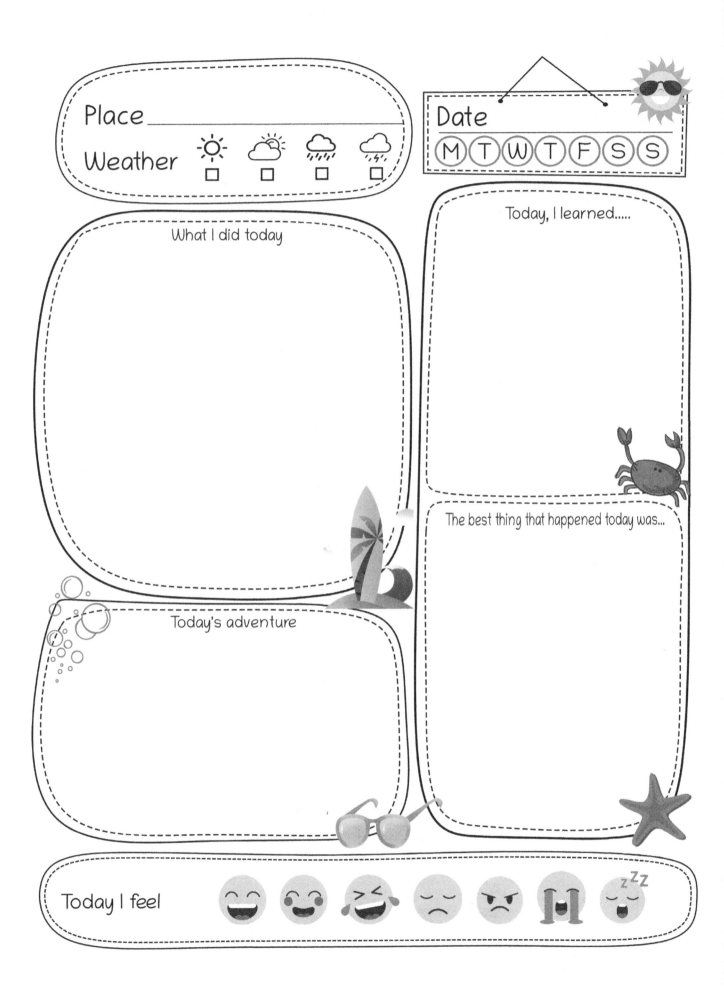

Place _____

Weather ☀ ☁ 🌧 🌧
        □ □ □ □

Date _____
M T W T F S S

What I did today

Today, I learned......

The best thing that happened today was...

Today's adventure

Today I feel

My favorite boardgame is....

My favorite thing to do is....

My favorite person is....

Place _____

Weather ☀ ⛅ 🌧 ⛈
□ □ □ □

Date _____
M T W T F S S

What I did today

Today, I learned.....

Today's adventure

The best thing that happened today was...

Today I feel   😄 😊 😆 😞 😠 😭 😴

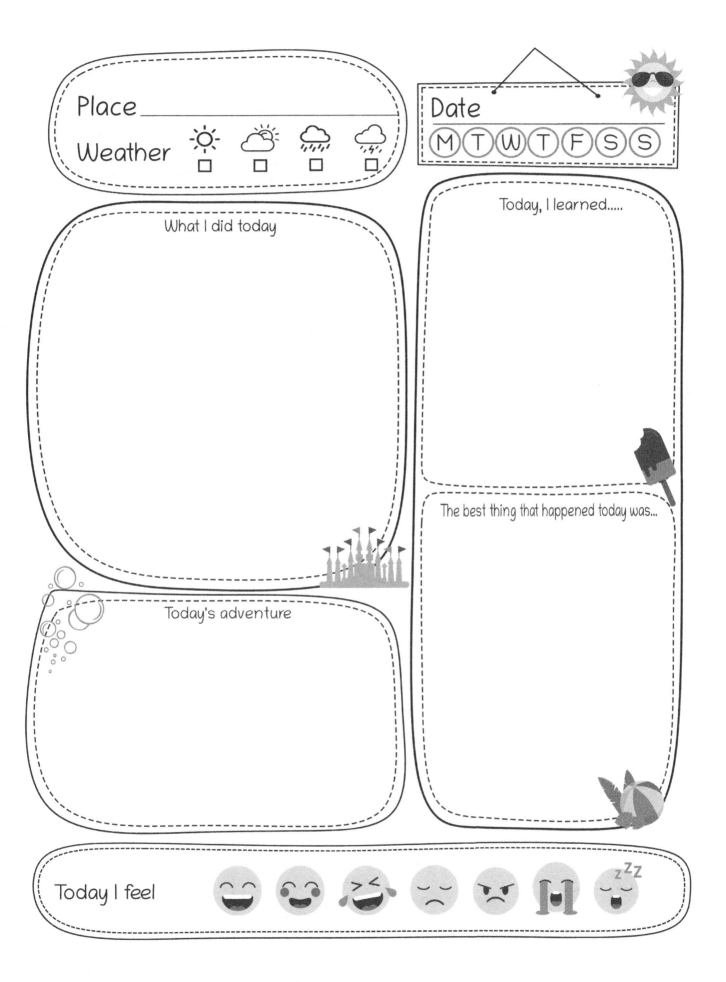

Place _____

Weather ☀ ☐ ⛅ ☐ 🌧 ☐ 🌦 ☐

Date _____
M T W T F S S

What I did today

Today, I learned.....

The best thing that happened today was...

Today's adventure

Today I feel

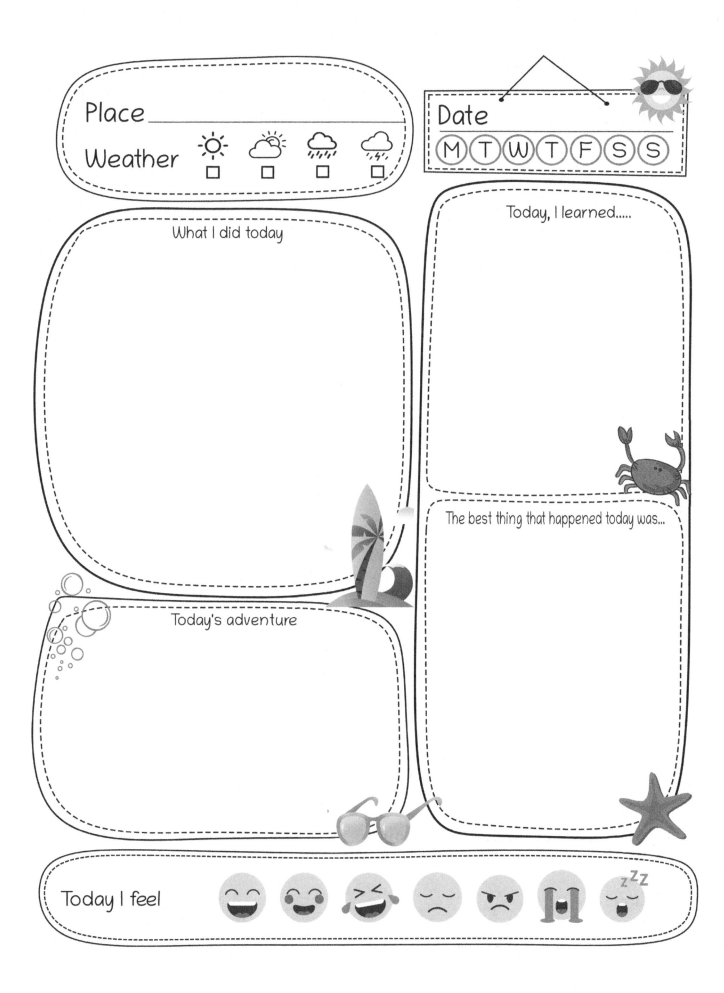

Place _____

Weather ☀ ☁ 🌧 ⛈
□ □ □ □

Date _____
M T W T F S S

What I did today

Today, I learned.....

The best thing that happened today was...

Today's adventure

Today I feel

My favorite summer drink recipe:

Ingredients:

_____

_____

_____

_____

_____

_____

_____

Steps:

_____

_____

_____

_____

_____

_____

_____

(Can you come up with a really cool drink recipe? Ask a grown-up, if you need help making it!)

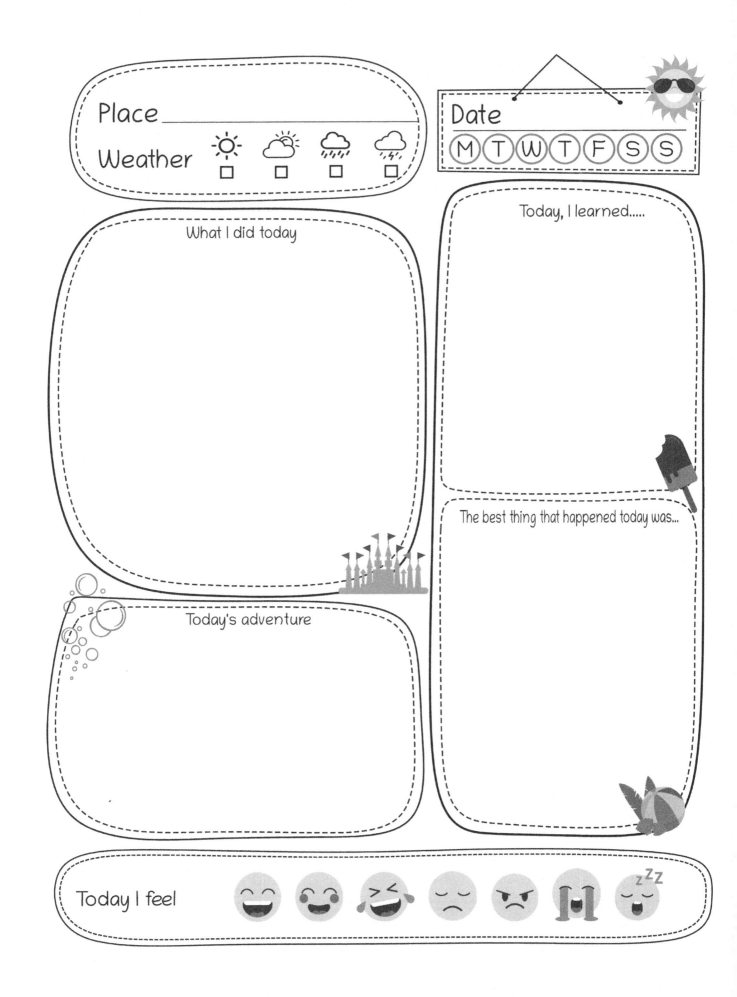

Place _____

Weather ☀ ⛅ 🌧 ⛈

Date _____
M T W T F S S

What I did today

Today, I learned......

The best thing that happened today was...

Today's adventure

Today I feel

Place _____

Weather ☀ 🌤 🌧 ⛈
☐ ☐ ☐ ☐

Date _____
Ⓜ Ⓣ Ⓦ Ⓣ Ⓕ Ⓢ Ⓢ

What I did today

Today, I learned.....

The best thing that happened today was...

Today's adventure

Today I feel 😄 😊 😆 😞 😠 😭 😴

My inventions :

Use this space to draw/design things that you would really like to invent. Use the opposite page to write/describe it in as much detail as you want to.....

My inventions :

_____

_____

_____

_____

_____

_____

_____

_____

_____

_____

_____

_____

_____

_____

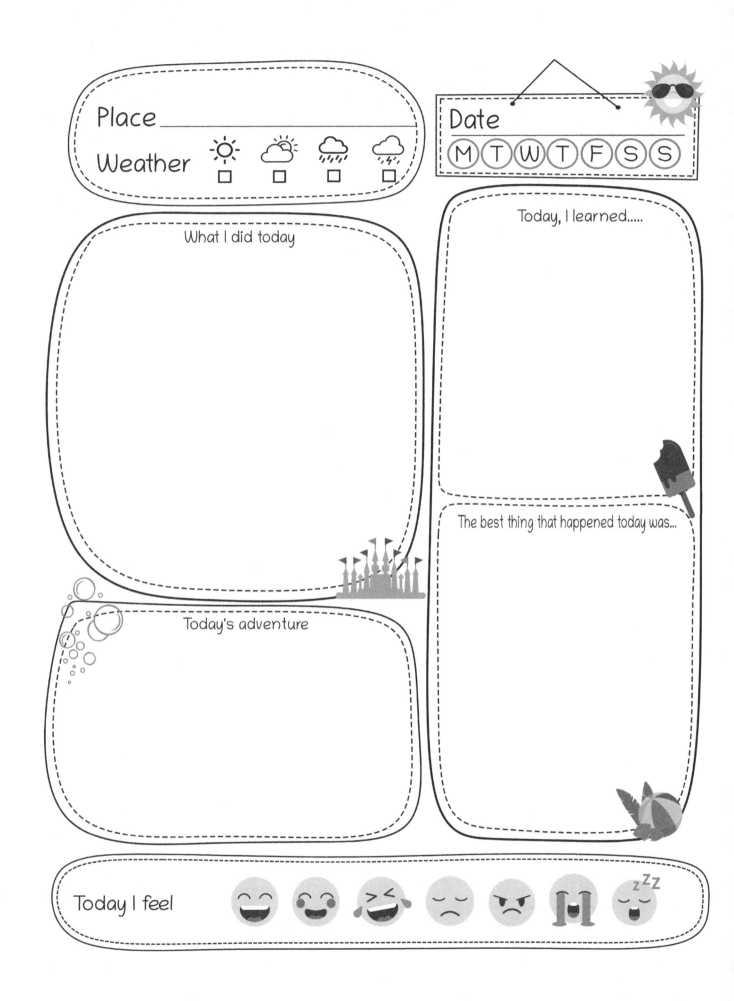

Place _____

Weather ☀ ⛅ 🌧 ⛈

Date _____

M T W T F S S

What I did today

Today, I learned.....

Today's adventure

The best thing that happened today was...

Today I feel 😄 😊 😆 😔 😠 😭 😴

Place _____

Weather

Date

M T W T F S S

What I did today

Today, I learned.....

The best thing that happened today was...

Today's adventure

Today I feel

My favorite camping story :

Have you been camping? What is your favorite camping memory? Draw or stick pictures and write about it. If you haven't been camping, can you make up a story about it?

My favorite camping story :

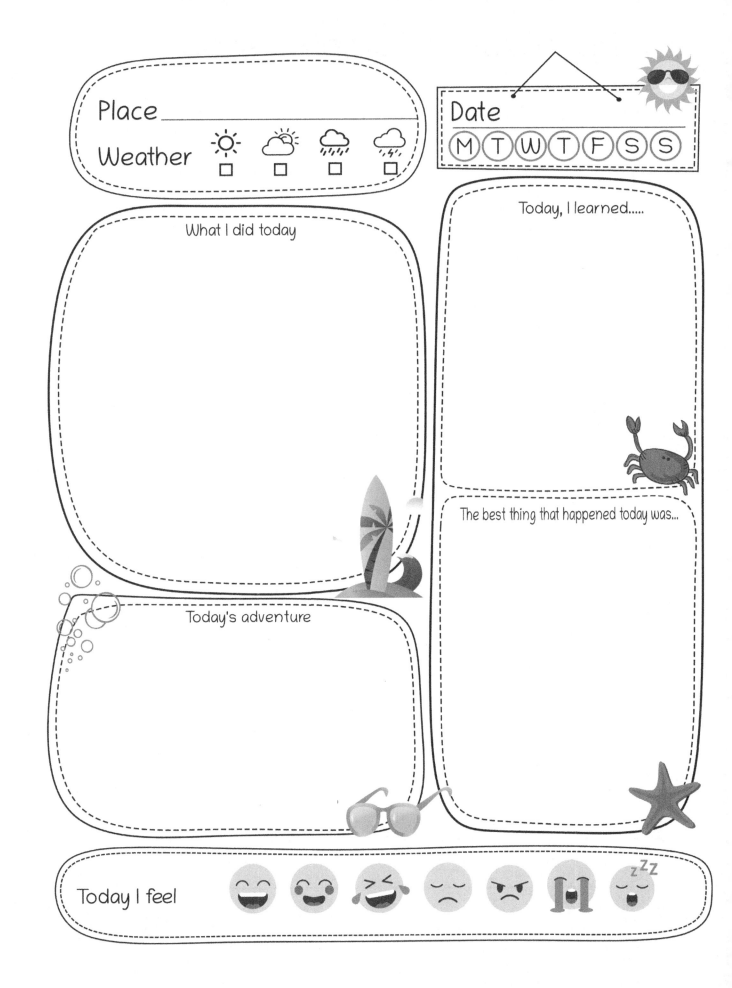

Place _____

Weather ☀ ⛅ 🌧 ⛈
☐ ☐ ☐ ☐

Date _____
Ⓜ Ⓣ Ⓦ Ⓣ Ⓕ Ⓢ Ⓢ

What I did today

Today, I learned.....

The best thing that happened today was...

Today's adventure

Today I feel

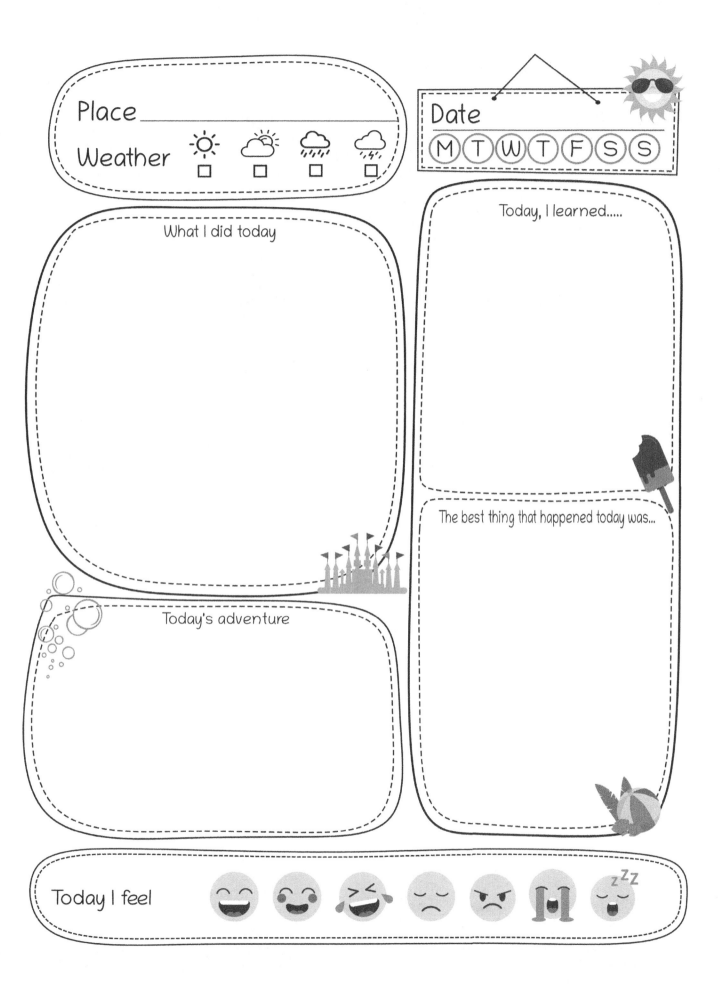

Place _____

Weather ☀ ☐ ⛅ ☐ 🌧 ☐ 🌧 ☐

Date _____
M T W T F S S

What I did today

Today, I learned......

The best thing that happened today was...

Today's adventure

Today I feel 😄 😌 😆 🙁 😠 😢 😴

Place _____

Weather

Date _____

M T W T F S S

What I did today

Today, I learned......

The best thing that happened today was...

Today's adventure

Today I feel

My best friend is:

I like him/her because he/she is

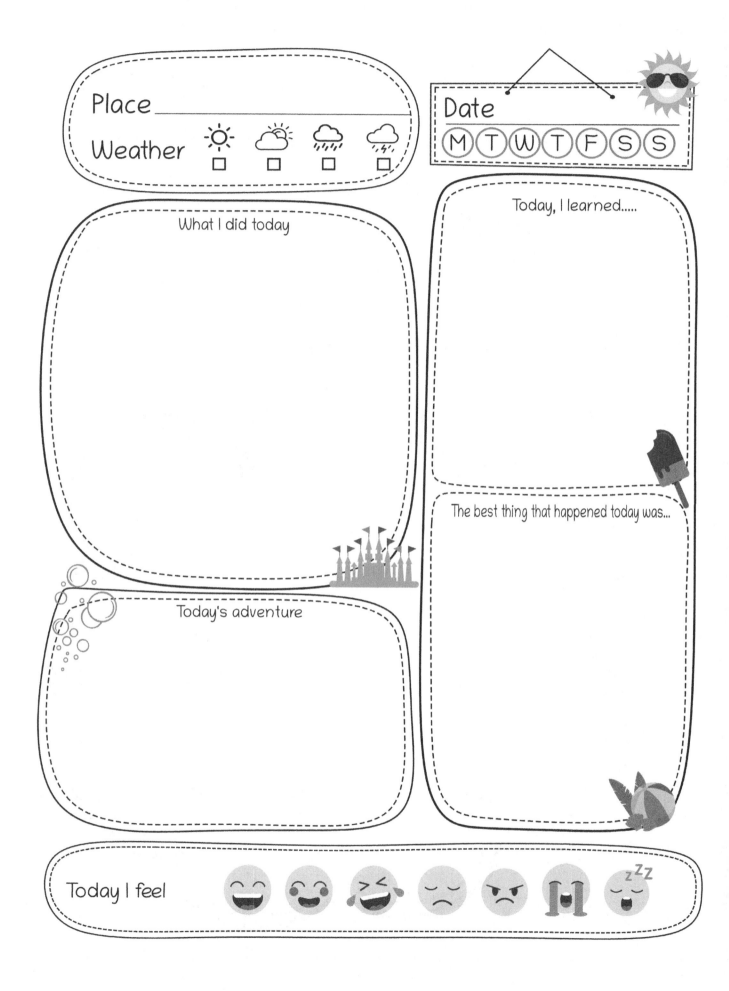

Place _____

Weather ☀ ⛅ 🌧 ⛈

Date _____
M T W T F S S

What I did today

Today, I learned......

The best thing that happened today was...

Today's adventure

Today I feel 😄 😋 😆 😞 😠 😭 😴

Place _____

Weather ☀ ☁ 🌧 ⛈
□ □ □ □

Date _____
M T W T F S S

What I did today

Today, I learned.....

Today's adventure

The best thing that happened today was...

Today I feel

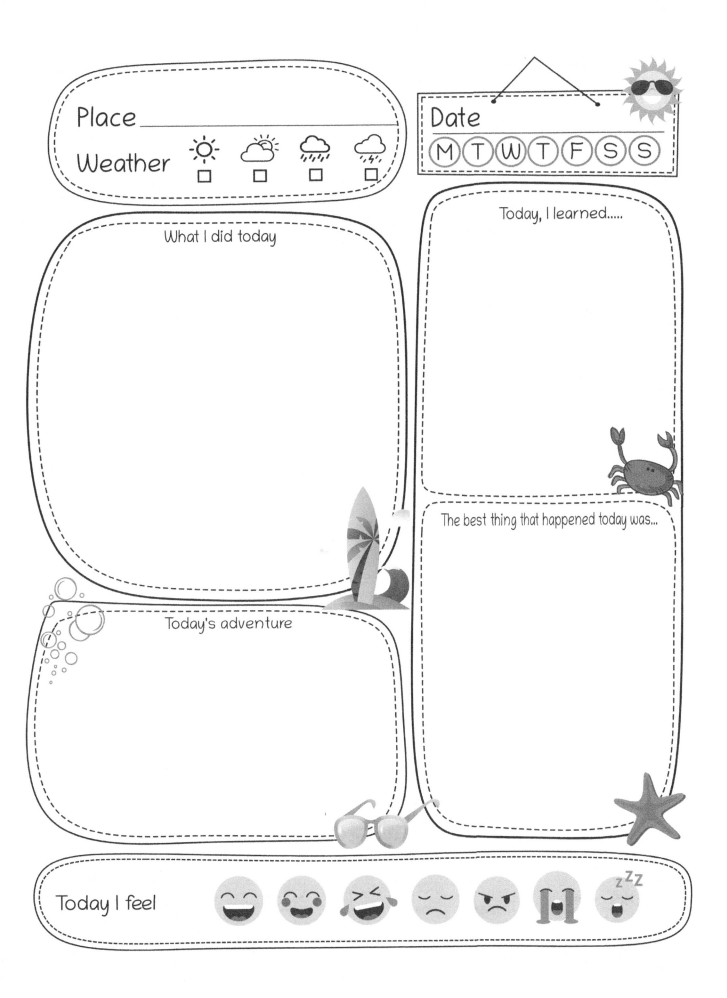

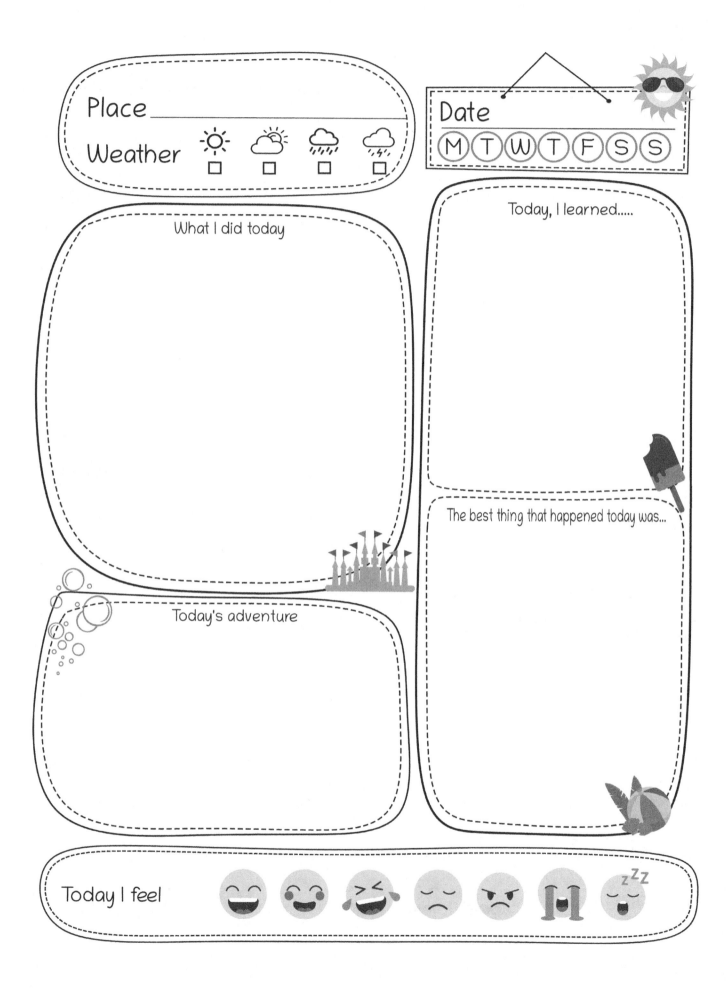

Place _____

Weather

Date

M T W T F S S

What I did today

Today, I learned.....

The best thing that happened today was...

Today's adventure

Today I feel

I think my best qualities are:

If I get mad/grumpy, this is what helps me calm down

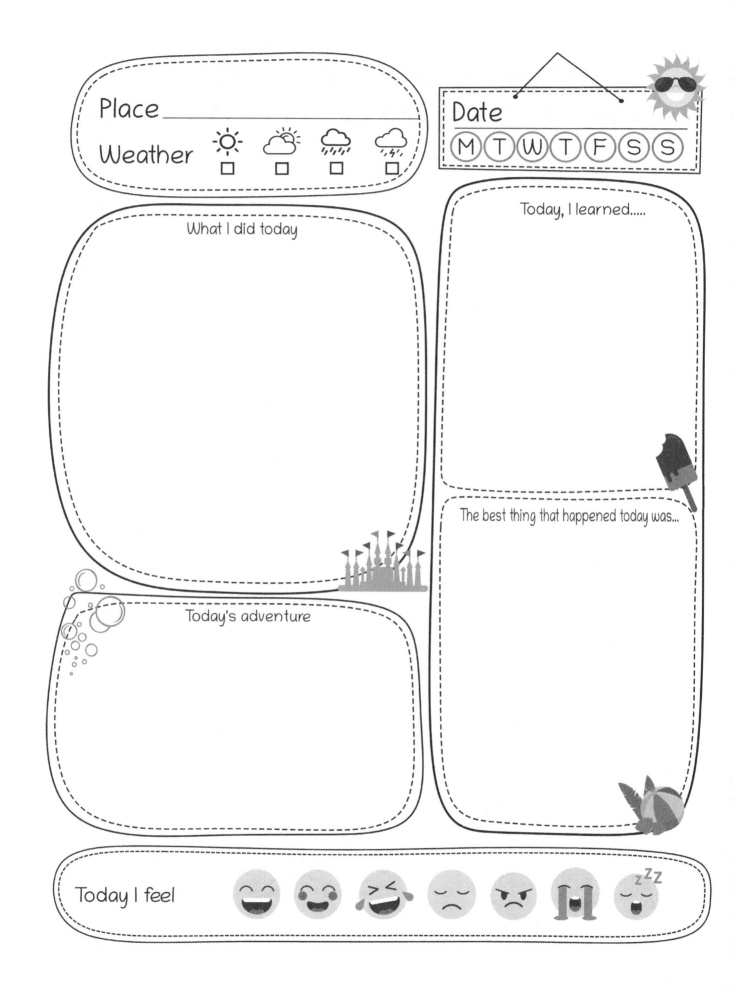

Place _____

Weather ☀ ⛅ 🌧 ⛈
☐ ☐ ☐ ☐

Date _____
Ⓜ Ⓣ Ⓦ Ⓣ Ⓕ Ⓢ Ⓢ

What I did today

Today, I learned......

The best thing that happened today was...

Today's adventure

Today I feel

Place _____

Weather ☀ ⛅ 🌧 ☁
□ □ □ □

Date _____
Ⓜ Ⓣ Ⓦ Ⓣ Ⓕ Ⓢ Ⓢ

What I did today

Today, I learned.....

The best thing that happened today was...

Today's adventure

Today I feel 😄 😊 😆 😞 😠 😭 😴

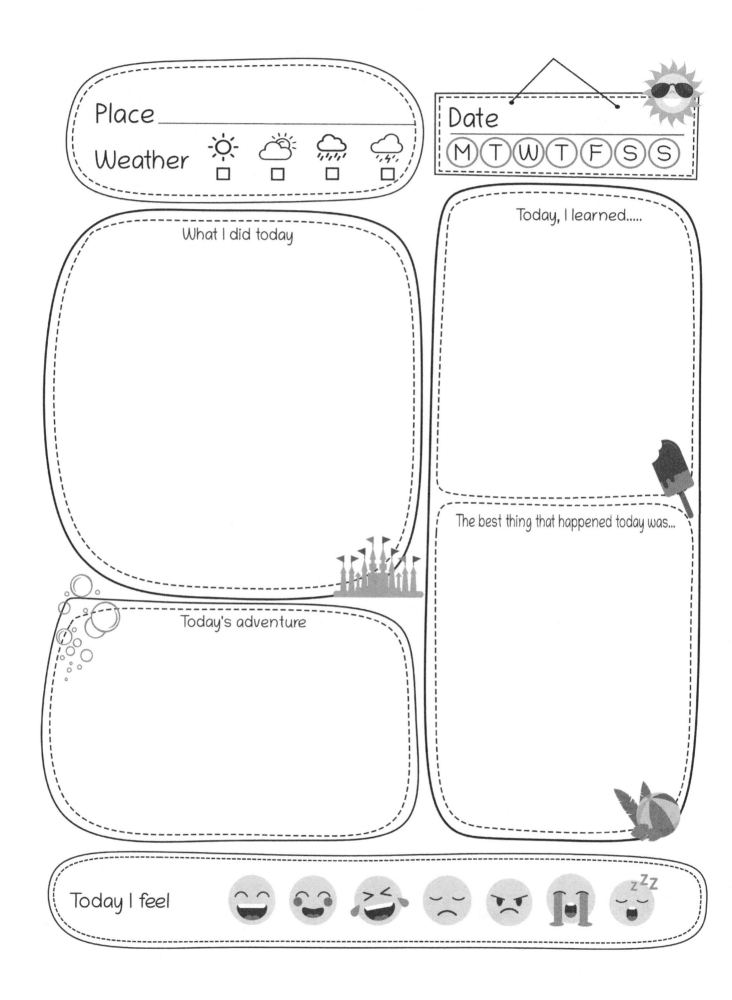

Place _____

Weather ☀️ ⛅ 🌧️ ☁️

Date _____
M T W T F S S

What I did today

Today, I learned.....

The best thing that happened today was...

Today's adventure

Today I feel 😄 😊 😆 🙁 😠 😭 😴

My favorite book is

I like this book because...

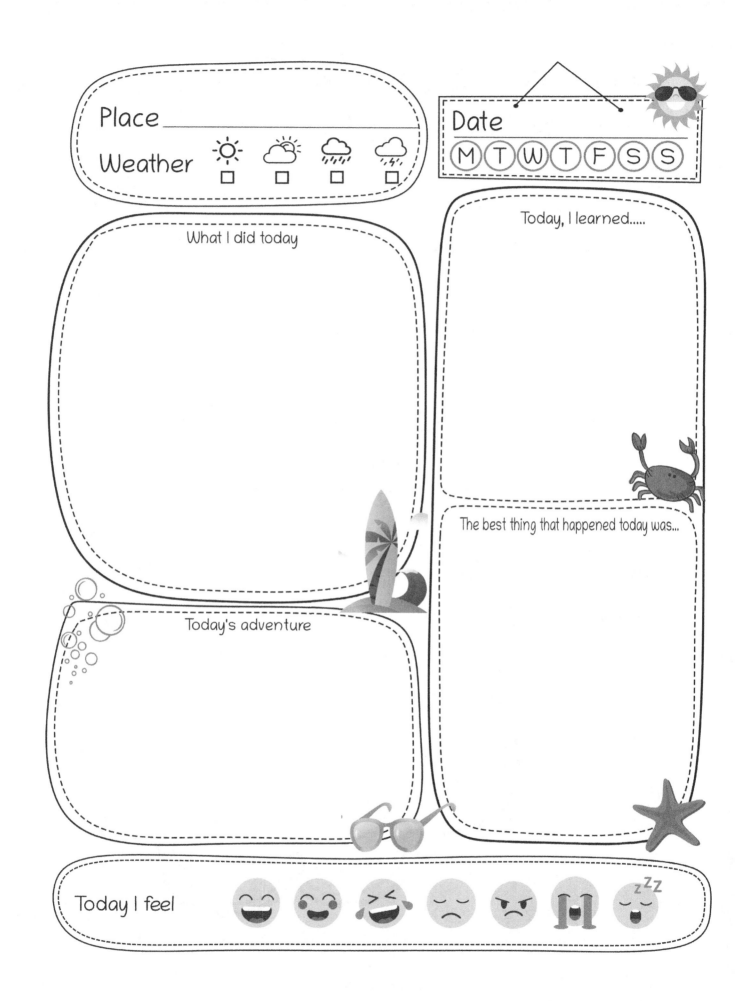

Place _____

Weather ☀ ⛅ 🌧 ⛈

Date _____
M T W T F S S

What I did today

Today, I learned.....

The best thing that happened today was...

Today's adventure

Today I feel

Place _____

Weather ☀ ⛅ 🌧 ⛈
□ □ □ □

Date
M T W T F S S

What I did today

Today, I learned.....

The best thing that happened today was...

Today's adventure

Today I feel 😄 😊 😆 😔 😠 😭 😴

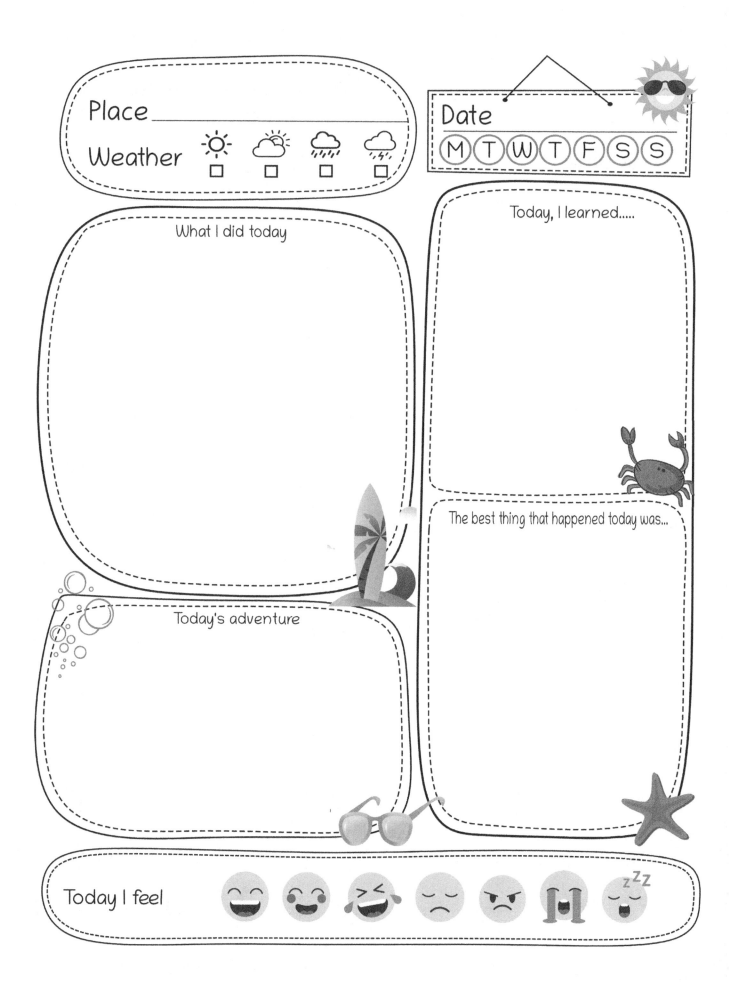

Place _____

Weather ☀ ⛅ 🌧 ⛈

Date _____
M T W T F S S

What I did today

Today, I learned.....

Today's adventure

The best thing that happened today was...

Today I feel

My backyard water-park...

If you could turn your backyard into a water-park, what would it look like?

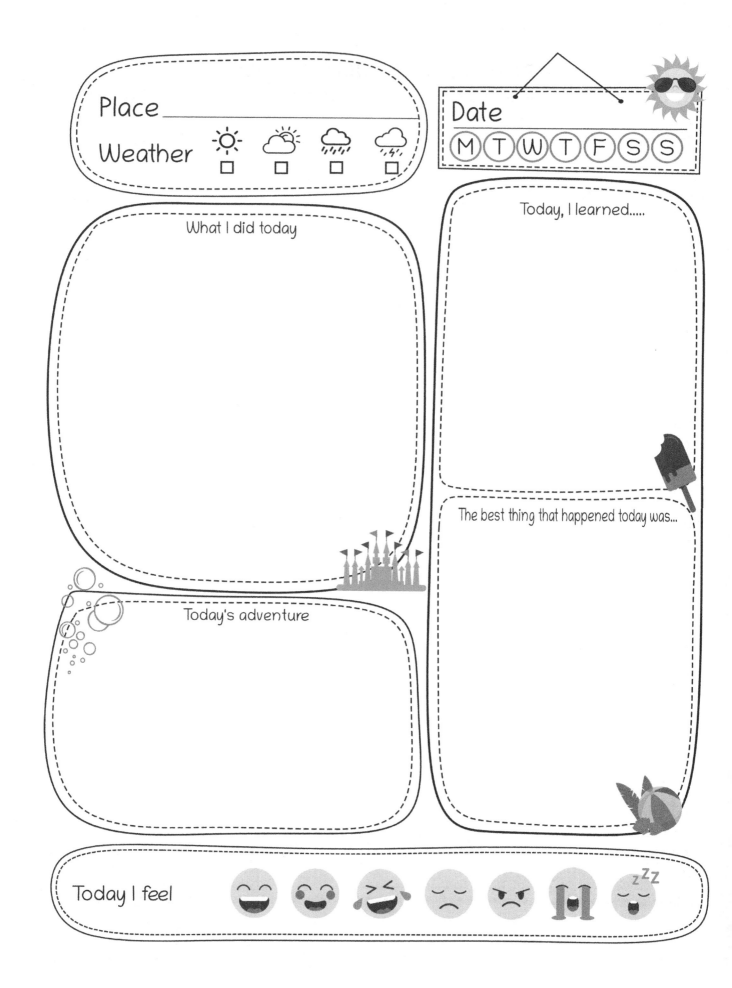

Place _____

Weather ☀ ⛅ 🌧 ⛈

Date _____
M T W T F S S

What I did today

Today, I learned......

Today's adventure

The best thing that happened today was...

Today I feel

Place _____

Weather ☀ ⛅ 🌧 ☁

Date
M T W T F S S

What I did today

Today, I learned.....

The best thing that happened today was...

Today's adventure

Today I feel 😄 😊 😂 😔 😠 😭 😴

My nature walk discoveries

Did you find anything interesting on one of your nature walks? Take a picture and stick it in the space here. Write about your walk and your discoveries on the opposite page.

My nature walk discoveries

Place _____

Weather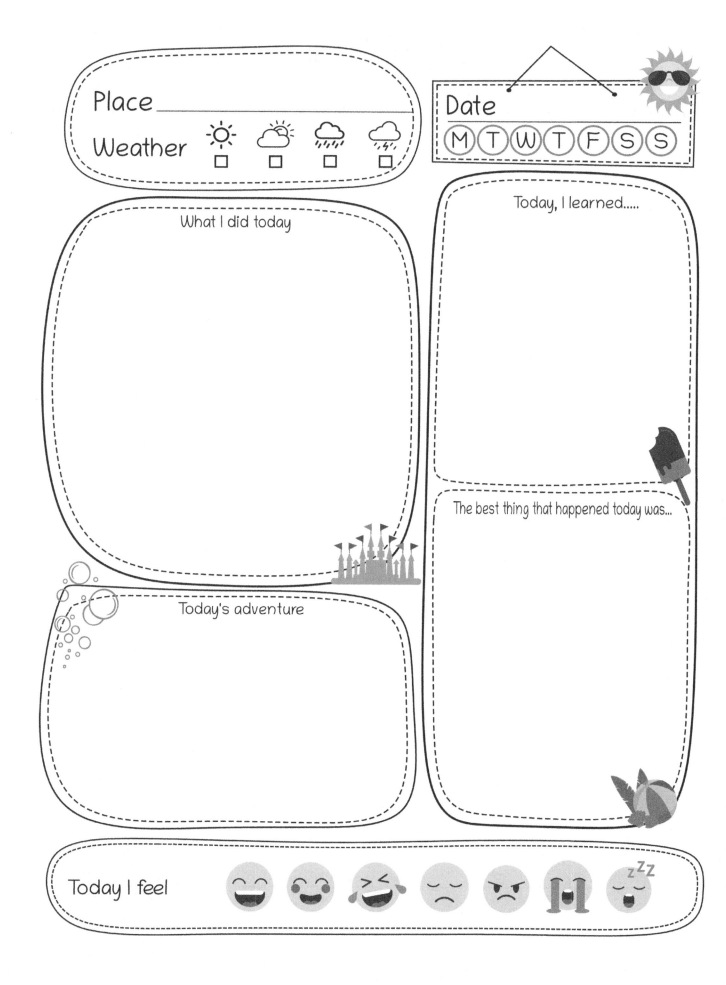

Date

M T W T F S S

What I did today

Today, I learned......

Today's adventure

The best thing that happened today was...

Today I feel

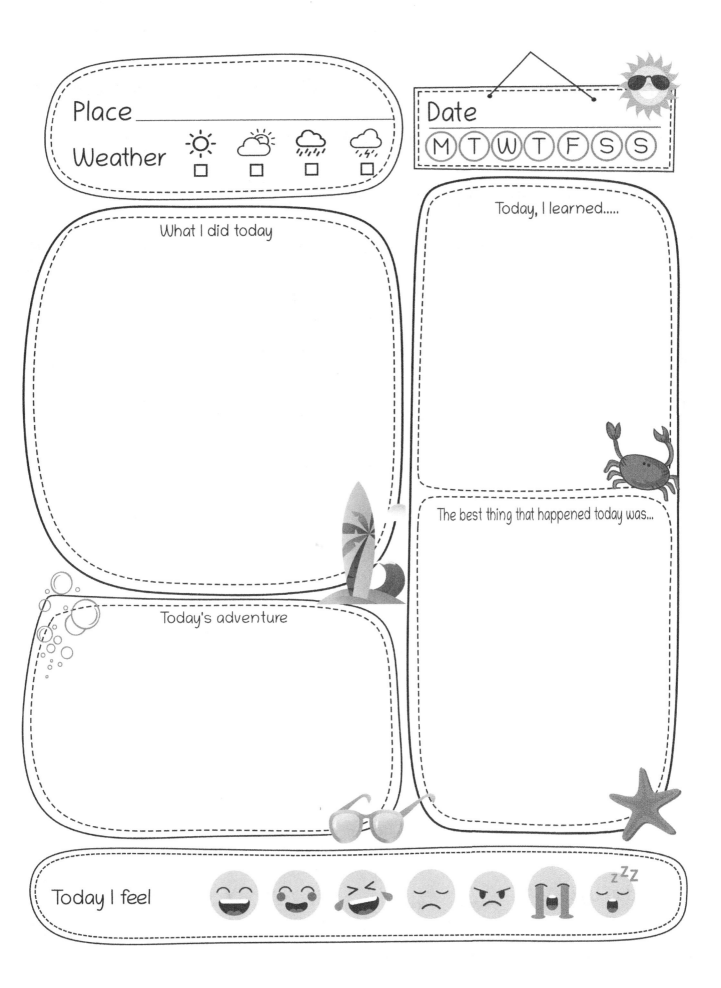

Place _____

Weather

Date

M T W T F S S

What I did today

Today, I learned.....

The best thing that happened today was...

Today's adventure

Today I feel

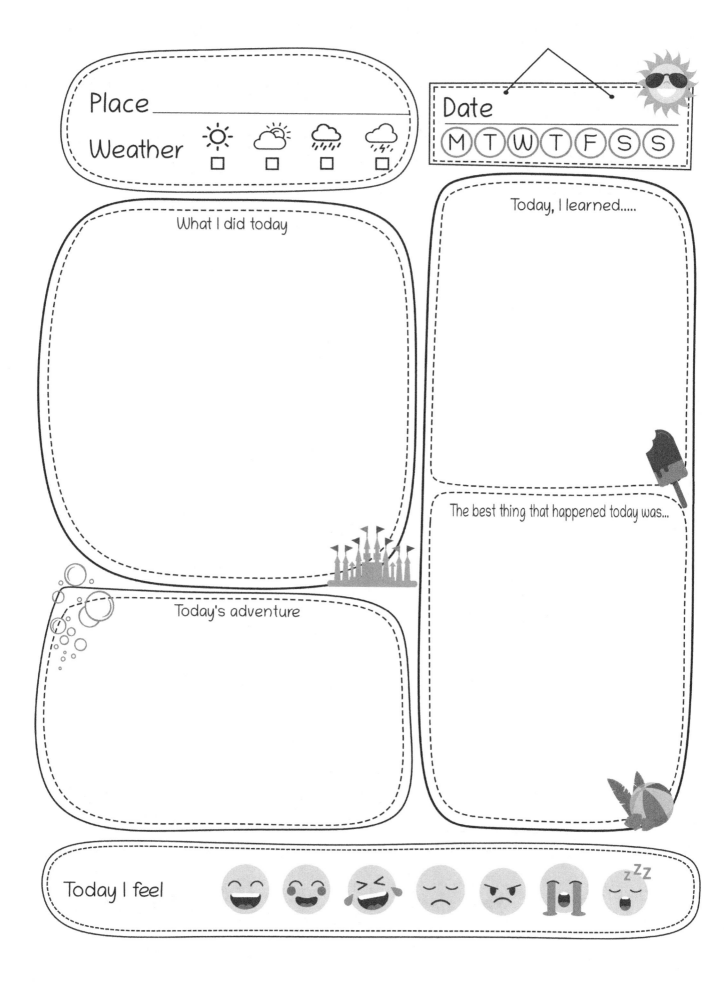

Place _____
Weather

Date
M T W T F S S

What I did today

Today, I learned.....

The best thing that happened today was...

Today's adventure

Today I feel

Place _____

Weather ☀ ⛅ 🌧 ☁
□ □ □ □

Date _____
Ⓜ Ⓣ Ⓦ Ⓣ Ⓕ Ⓢ Ⓢ

What I did today

Today, I learned.....

Today's adventure

The best thing that happened today was...

Today I feel   😄 😊 😆 😔 😠 😭 😴

My ideal pet

Can you think of an imaginary animal that you would love to have as a pet? Draw your sketch here and use the opposite page to describe what that pet would be like and why would it make a great pet?

What my ideal pet would be like....

_____

_____

_____

_____

_____

_____

_____

_____

_____

_____

_____

_____

_____

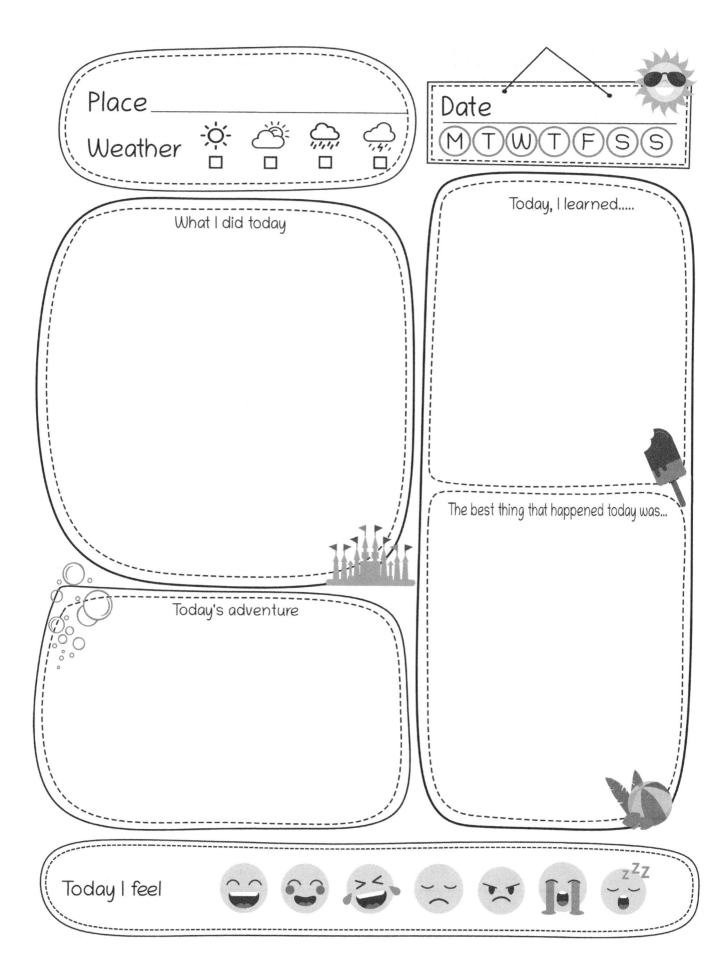

Place _____

Weather ☀ ☁ 🌧 ⛈

Date _____

M T W T F S S

What I did today

Today, I learned.....

The best thing that happened today was...

Today's adventure

Today I feel

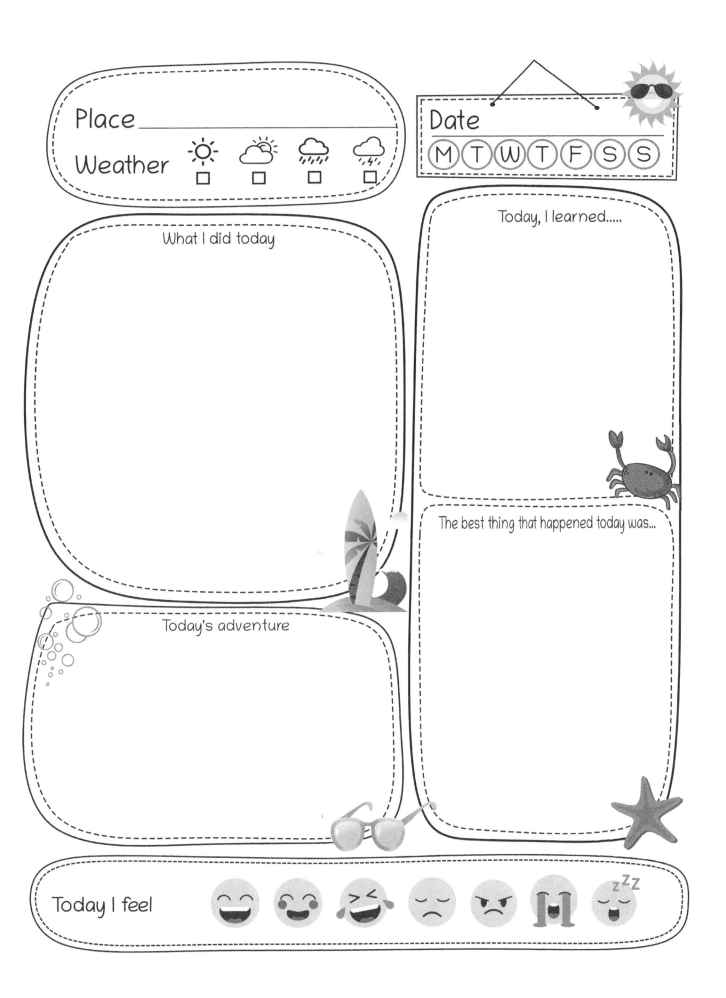

Place _____

Weather ☀ ☁ 🌧 ⛅

Date

M T W T F S S

What I did today

Today, I learned......

The best thing that happened today was...

Today's adventure

Today I feel

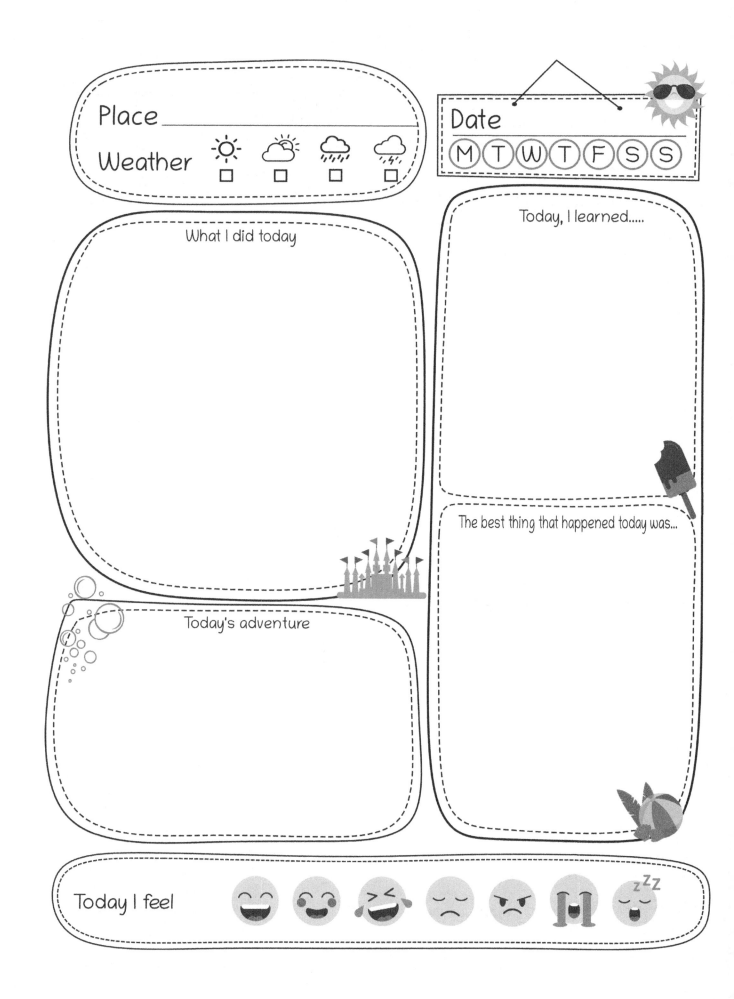

Place _____

Weather ☀ ⛅ 🌧 ⛈
□ □ □ □

Date _____
Ⓜ Ⓣ Ⓦ Ⓣ Ⓕ Ⓢ Ⓢ

What I did today

Today, I learned.....

The best thing that happened today was...

Today's adventure

Today I feel 😄 😊 😆 😔 😠 😭 😴

Place _____

Weather ☐ ☐ ☐ ☐

Date _____

M T W T F S S

What I did today

Today, I learned......

The best thing that happened today was...

Today's adventure

Today I feel

My favorite season is

My least favorite season is

Here is why....

Talk about why you like one season and what you don't like about the other.

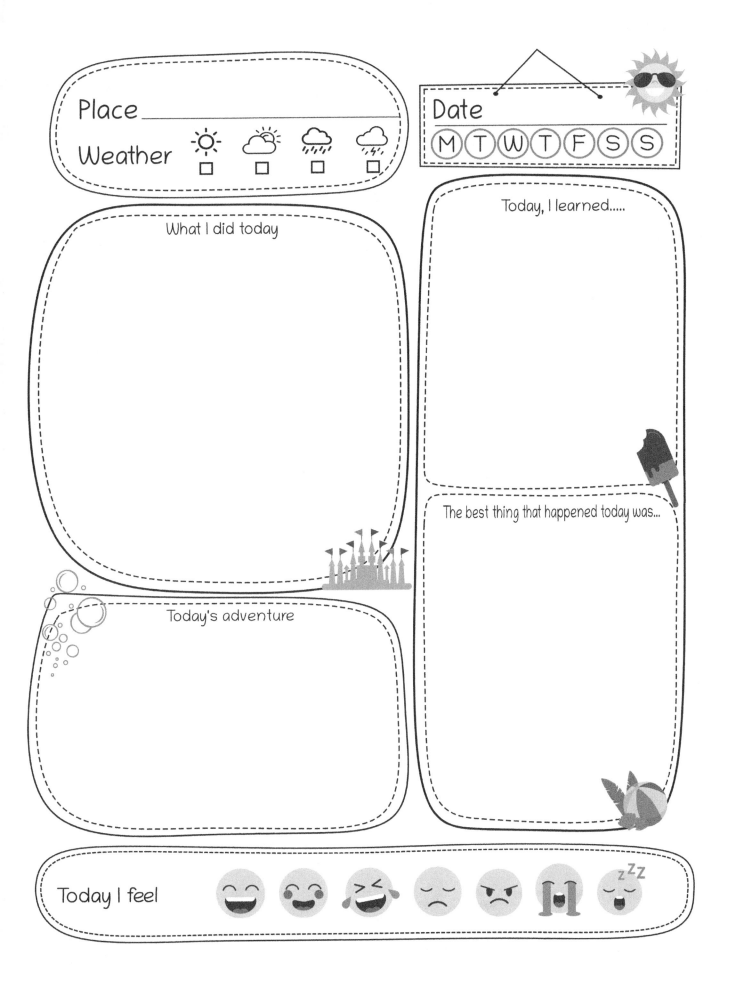

Place _____

Weather ☀ ⛅ 🌧 ☁

Date _____
Ⓜ Ⓣ Ⓦ Ⓣ Ⓕ Ⓢ Ⓢ

What I did today

Today, I learned.....

The best thing that happened today was...

Today's adventure

Today I feel

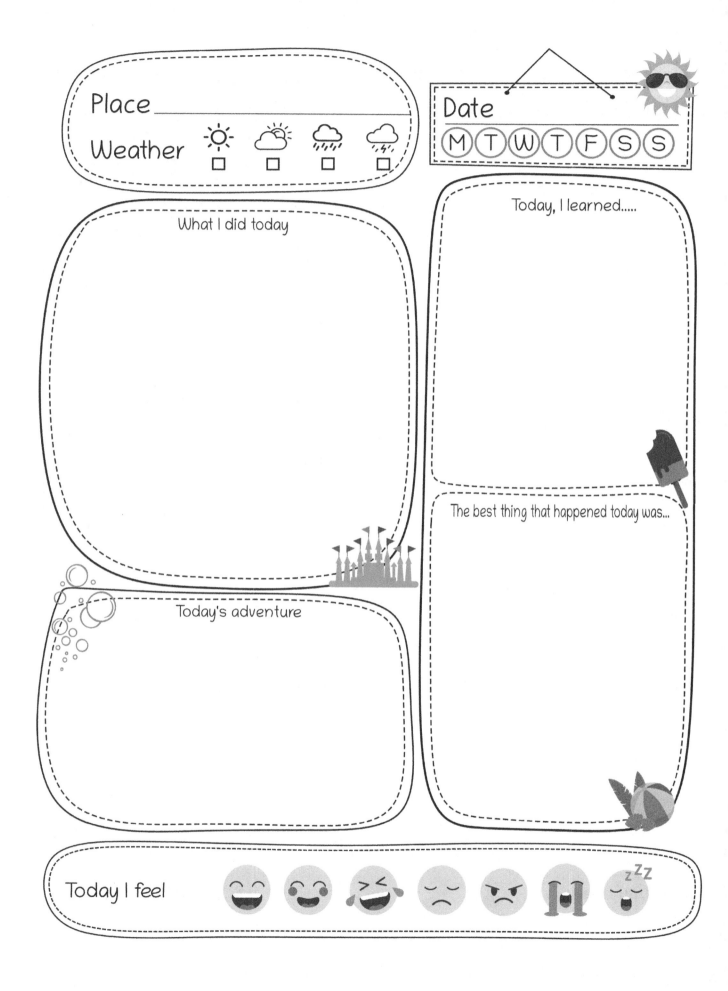

Place _____

Weather ☀ ⛅ 🌧 ⛈

Date _____

M T W T F S S

What I did today

Today, I learned......

The best thing that happened today was...

Today's adventure

Today I feel

Place _____

Weather ☀️ ☐ ⛅ ☐ 🌧️ ☐ 🌧️ ☐

Date _____
Ⓜ Ⓣ Ⓦ Ⓣ Ⓕ Ⓢ Ⓢ

What I did today

Today, I learned.....

The best thing that happened today was...

Today's adventure

Today I feel

My very own ice-cream recipe :

Ingredients:

_____

_____

_____

_____

_____

_____

_____

Steps:

_____

_____

_____

_____

_____

_____

_____

July is national ice-cream month. Can you come up with your very own flavor of ice-cream?

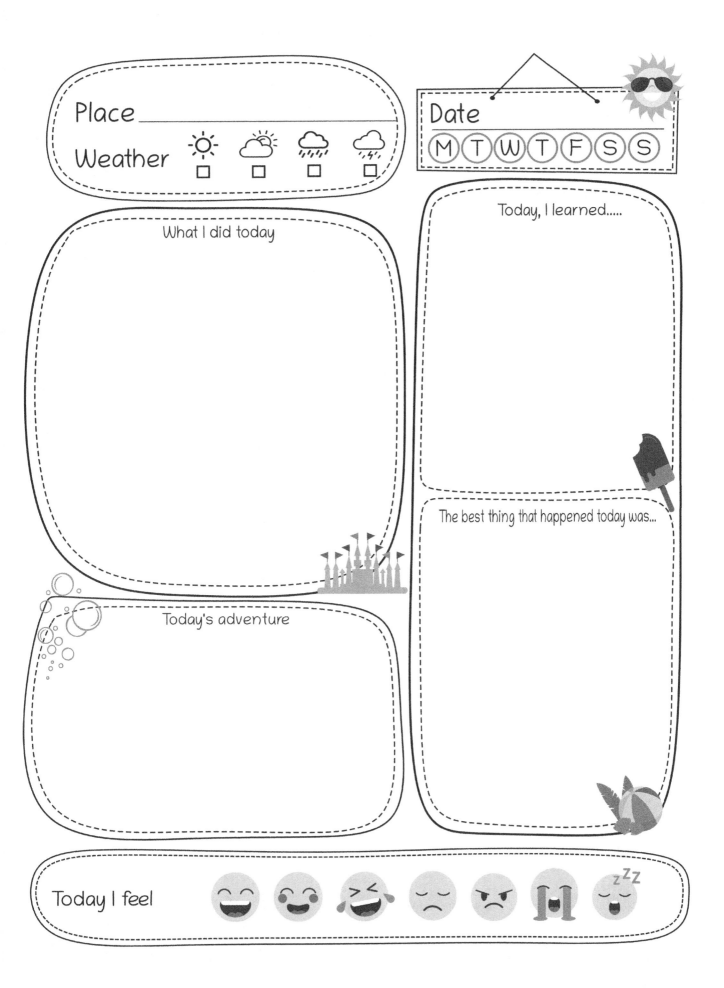

Place _____

Weather ☀ ⛅ 🌧 ☁
□ □ □ □

Date
M T W T F S S

What I did today

Today, I learned......

The best thing that happened today was...

Today's adventure

Today I feel 😄 😊 😂 😔 😠 😭 😴

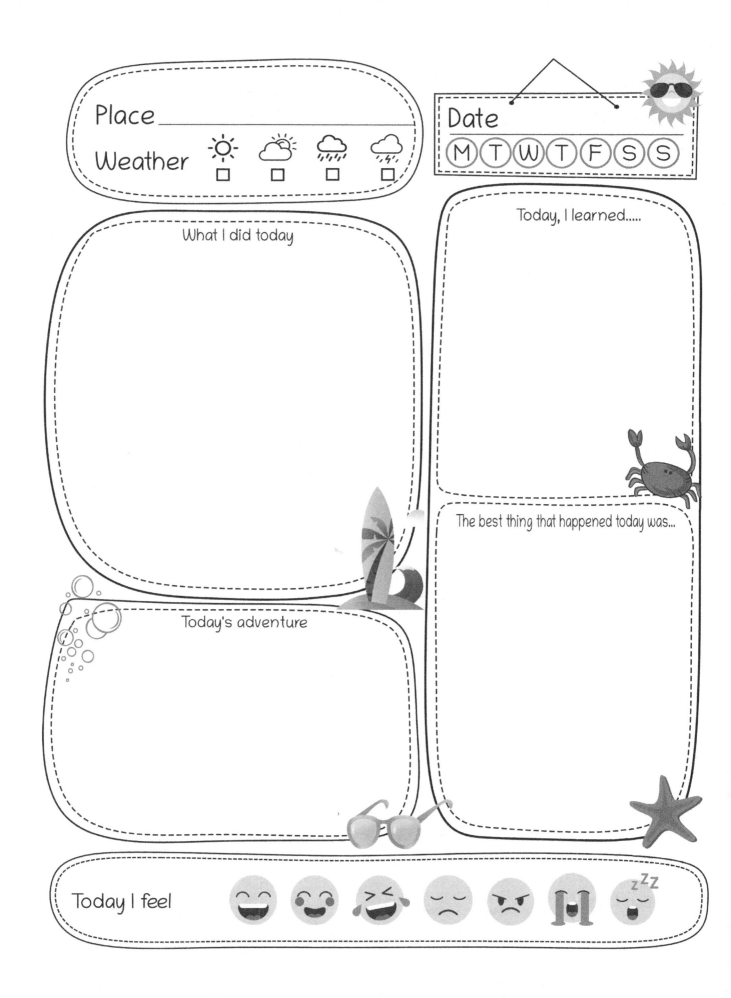

Place _____

Weather ☀ ⛅ 🌧 ☁
☐ ☐ ☐ ☐

Date _____
M T W T F S S

What I did today

Today, I learned.....

The best thing that happened today was...

Today's adventure

Today I feel

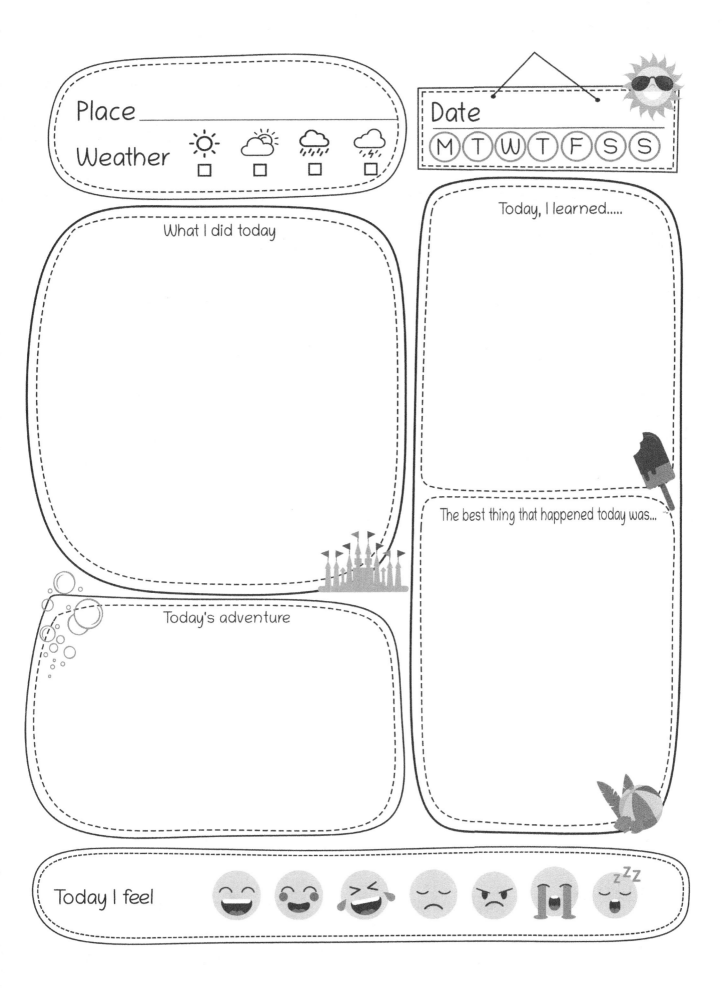

Place _____

Weather ☀ ⛅ 🌧 🌧
☐ ☐ ☐ ☐

Date _____
Ⓜ Ⓣ Ⓦ Ⓣ Ⓕ Ⓢ Ⓢ

What I did today

Today, I learned.....

The best thing that happened today was...

Today's adventure

Today I feel

Place _____

Weather ☀️☐ ⛅☐ 🌧️☐ ⛈️☐

Date _____

(M)(T)(W)(T)(F)(S)(S)

What I did today

Today, I learned.....

The best thing that happened today was...

Today's adventure

Today I feel 😄 😊 😆 😞 😠 😭 😴

My favorite picnic place is

SUMMER

My favorite picnic food is

Here is who I
had love to have
the picnic with...

Place _____

Weather ☀️ ☐ ⛅ ☐ 🌧️ ☐ ⛈️ ☐

Date _____
Ⓜ Ⓣ Ⓦ Ⓣ Ⓕ Ⓢ Ⓢ

What I did today

Today, I learned......

The best thing that happened today was...

Today's adventure

Today I feel   😄 😊 😆 😔 😠 😭 😴

Place _____

Weather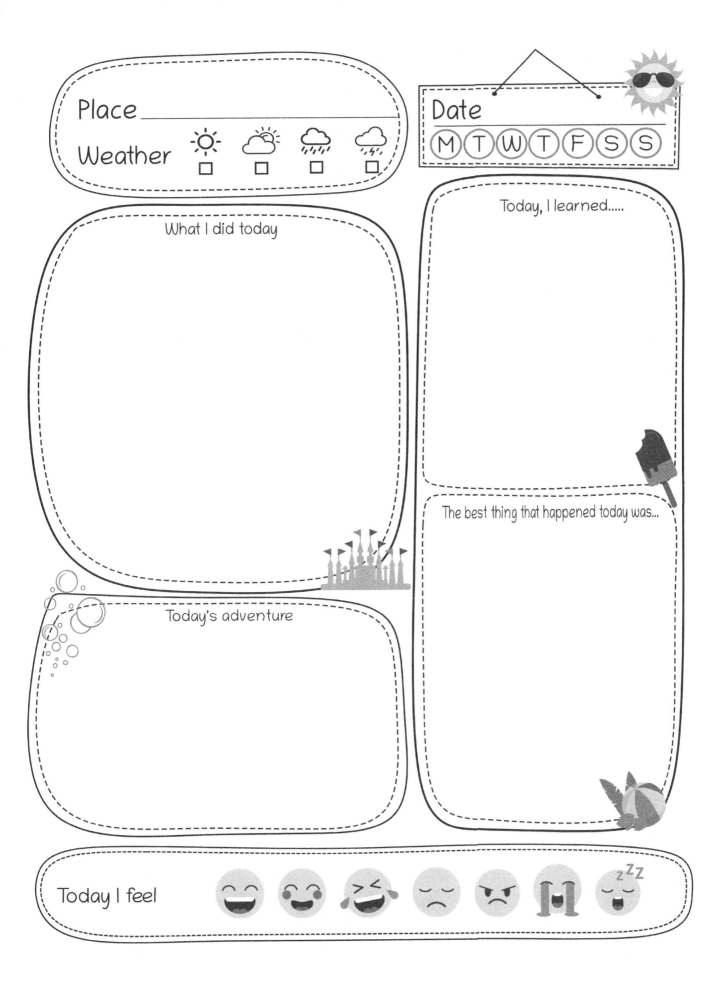

Date

M T W T F S S

What I did today

Today, I learned......

The best thing that happened today was...

Today's adventure

Today I feel

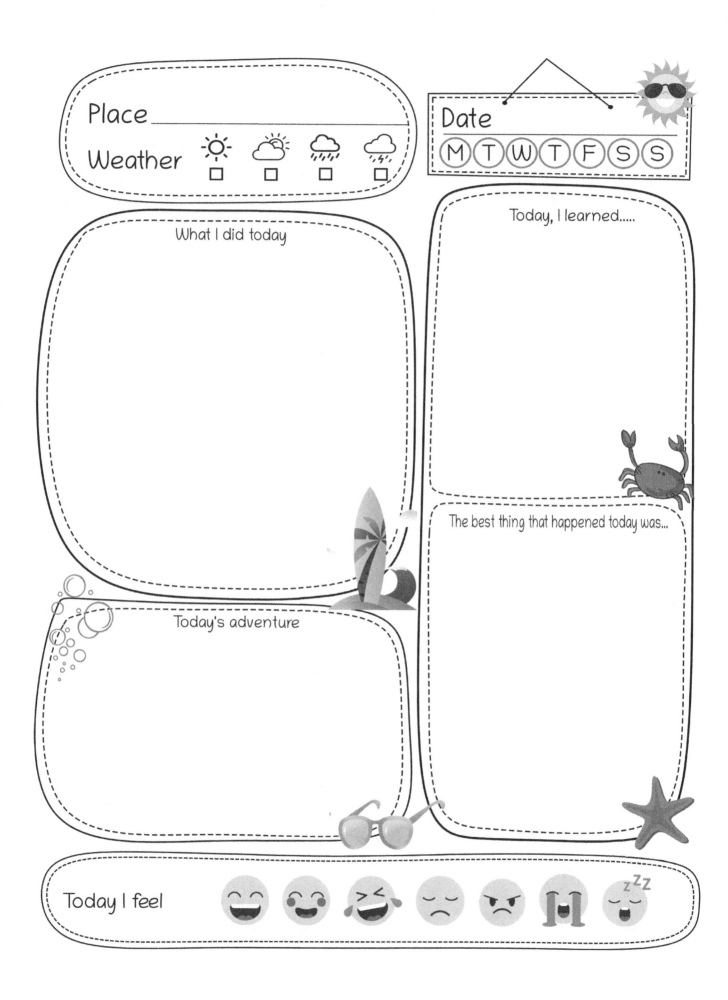

Place _____

Weather ☀ ⛅ 🌧 ⛈
□ □ □ □

Date
M T W T F S S

What I did today

Today, I learned.....

The best thing that happened today was...

Today's adventure

Today I feel

This is what I miss most about going to school

This is what I miss least about going to school

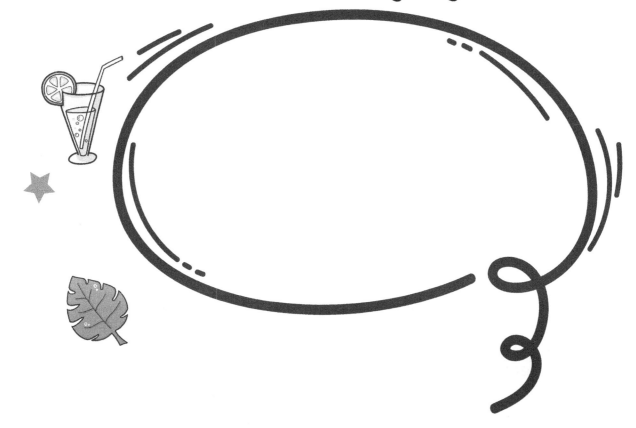

Place _____

Weather ☀ ⛅ 🌧 ⛈
□ □ □ □

Date _____
Ⓜ Ⓣ Ⓦ Ⓣ Ⓕ Ⓢ Ⓢ

What I did today

Today, I learned.....

Today's adventure

The best thing that happened today was...

Today I feel 😄 😊 😆 😔 😠 😭 😴

Place _____

Weather ☀ ⛅ 🌧 🌧

Date _____
M T W T F S S

What I did today

Today, I learned......

The best thing that happened today was...

Today's adventure

Today I feel

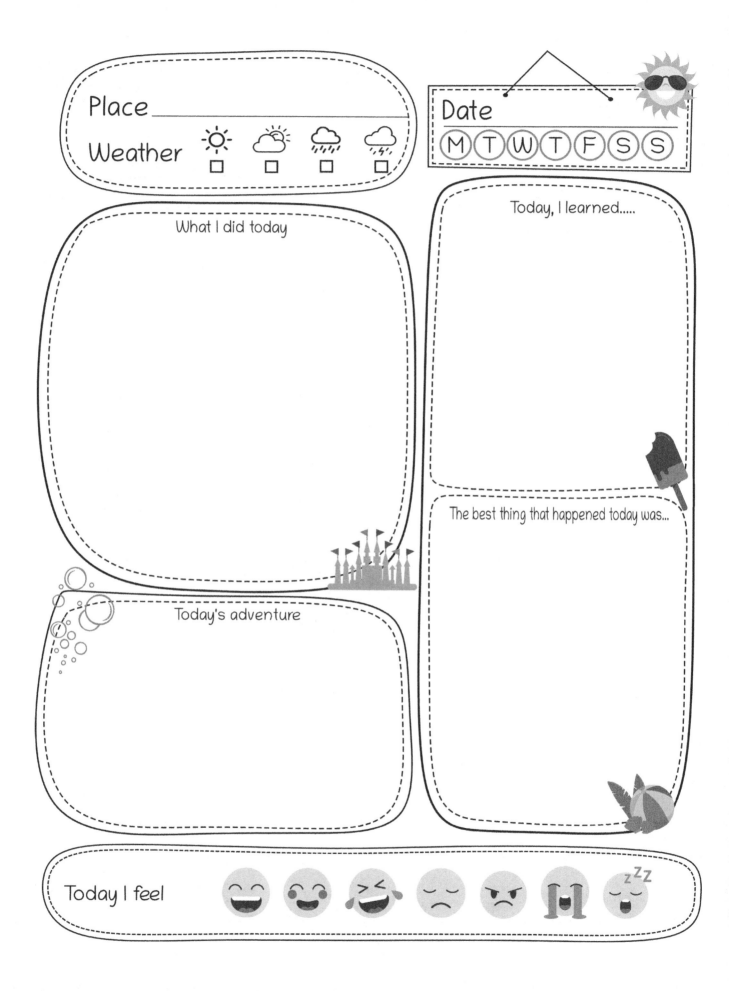

Place _____

Weather ☀ ☁ 🌧 ⛈
         ☐ ☐ ☐ ☐

Date _____
M T W T F S S

What I did today

Today, I learned......

The best thing that happened today was...

Today's adventure

Today I feel

Place

Weather

Date

M T W T F S S

What I did today

Today, I learned.....

The best thing that happened today was...

Today's adventure

Today I feel

All the gardening that I did ...

Did you do any gardening this summer? Click and stick pictures here, or draw the process. Use the opposite page to write about it.

Gardening- what I did and how I felt

_____

_____

_____

_____

_____

_____

_____

_____

_____

_____

_____

_____

_____

_____

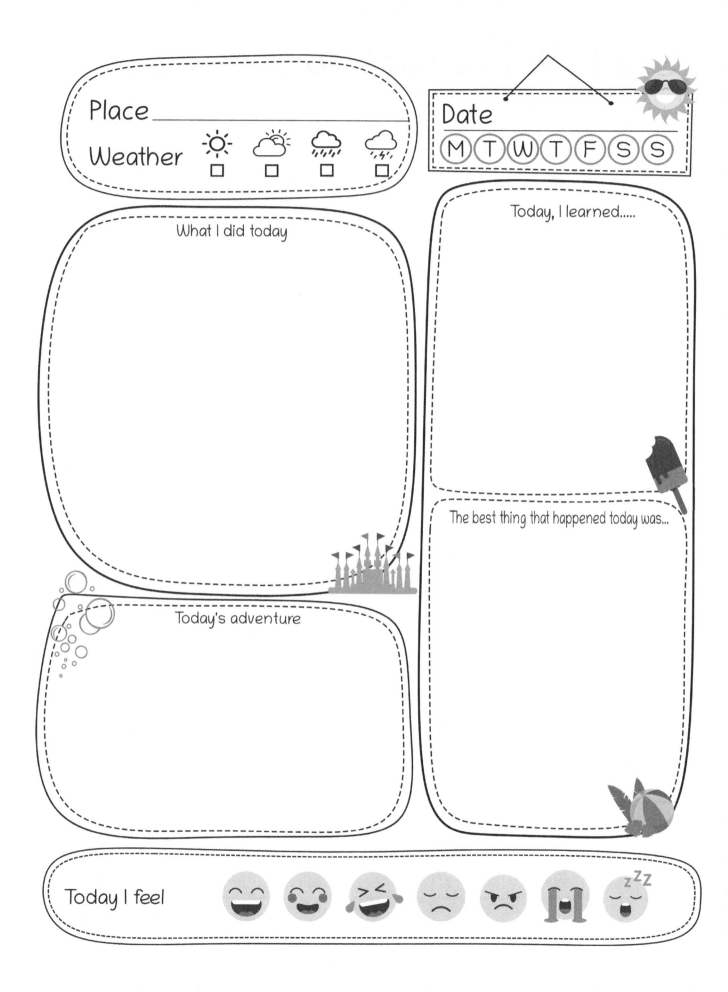

Place _____

Weather ☀ ☁ 🌧 ⛈
□ □ □ □

Date _____
M T W T F S S

What I did today

Today, I learned.....

The best thing that happened today was...

Today's adventure

Today I feel

Place _____

Weather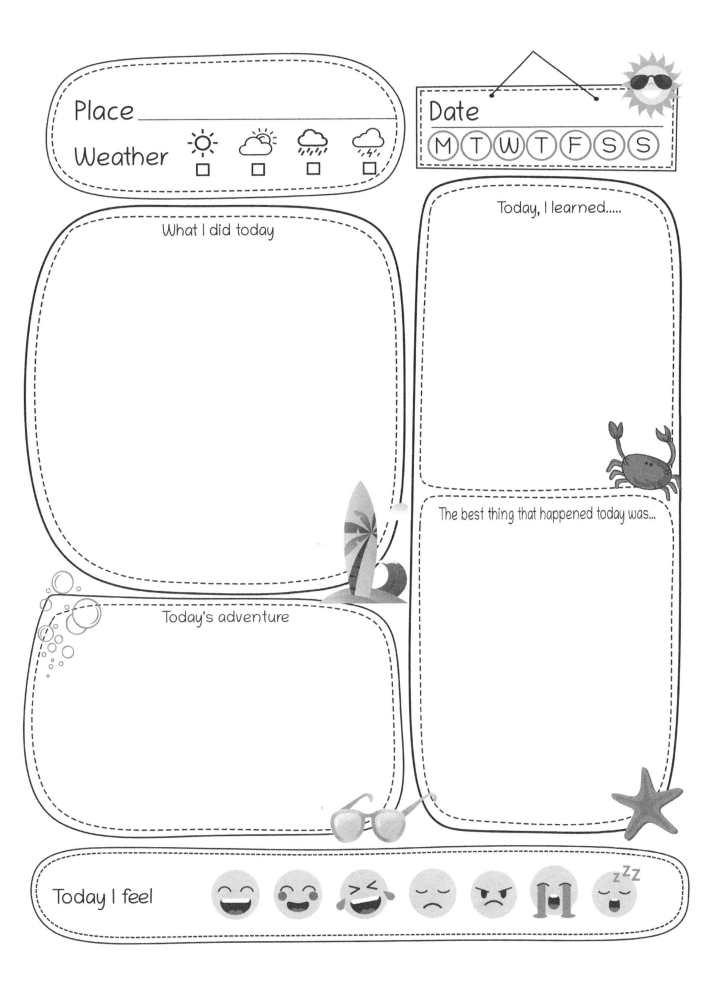

Date
(M)(T)(W)(T)(F)(S)(S)

What I did today

Today, I learned.....

The best thing that happened today was...

Today's adventure

Today I feel

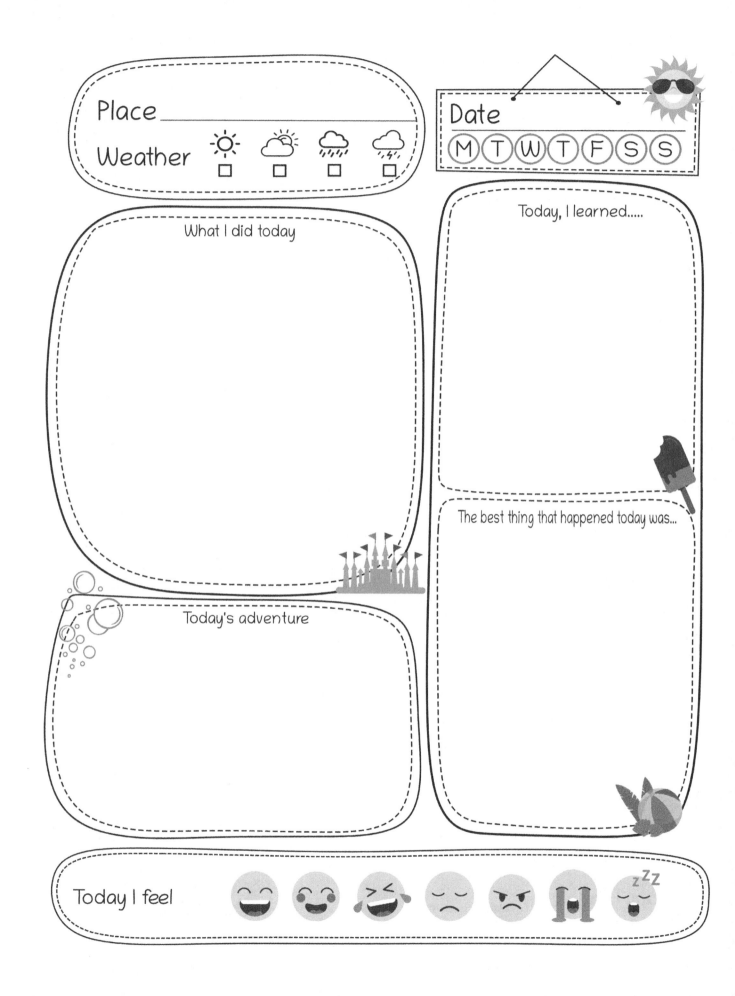

Place _____

Weather ☀ ☐   ⛅ ☐   🌧 ☐   🌧 ☐

Date
M T W T F S S

What I did today

Today, I learned......

Today's adventure

The best thing that happened today was...

Today I feel   😄 😊 😆 😞 😠 😭 😴

Place _____

Weather ☀ ⛅ 🌧 ⛈
         ☐ ☐ ☐ ☐

Date _____
M T W T F S S

What I did today

Today, I learned......

The best thing that happened today was...

Today's adventure

Today I feel

An example of
me doing
something nice
for someone...

An example of
when someone
did something
nice for me

Place _____

Weather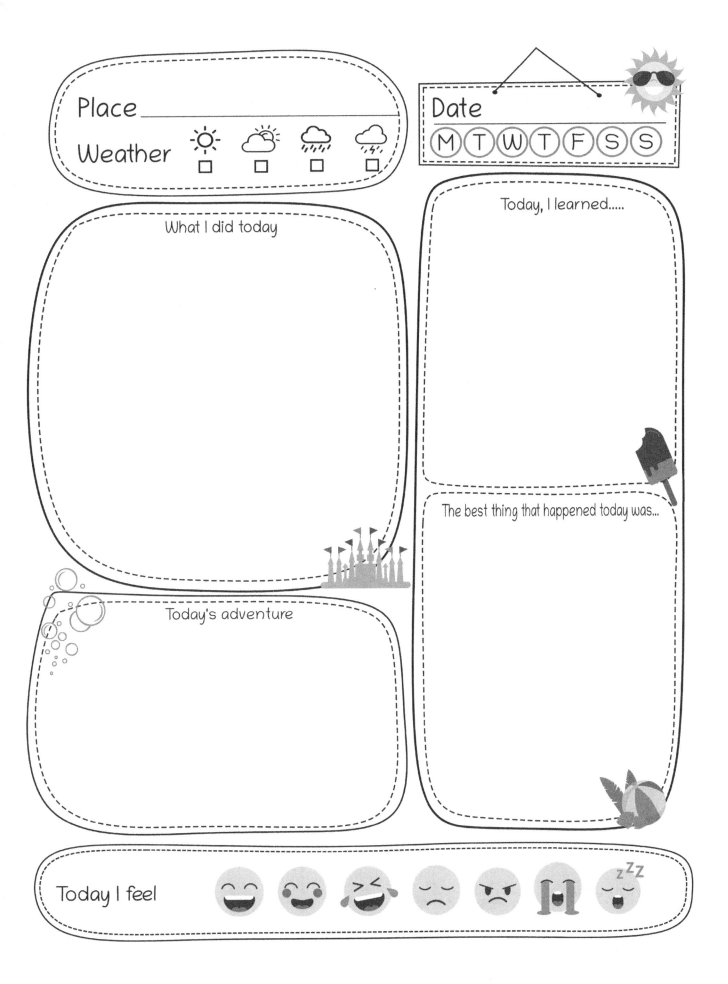

Date _____

M T W T F S S

What I did today

Today, I learned.....

The best thing that happened today was...

Today's adventure

Today I feel

Place _____

Weather

Date
M T W T F S S

What I did today

Today, I learned......

The best thing that happened today was...

Today's adventure

Today I feel

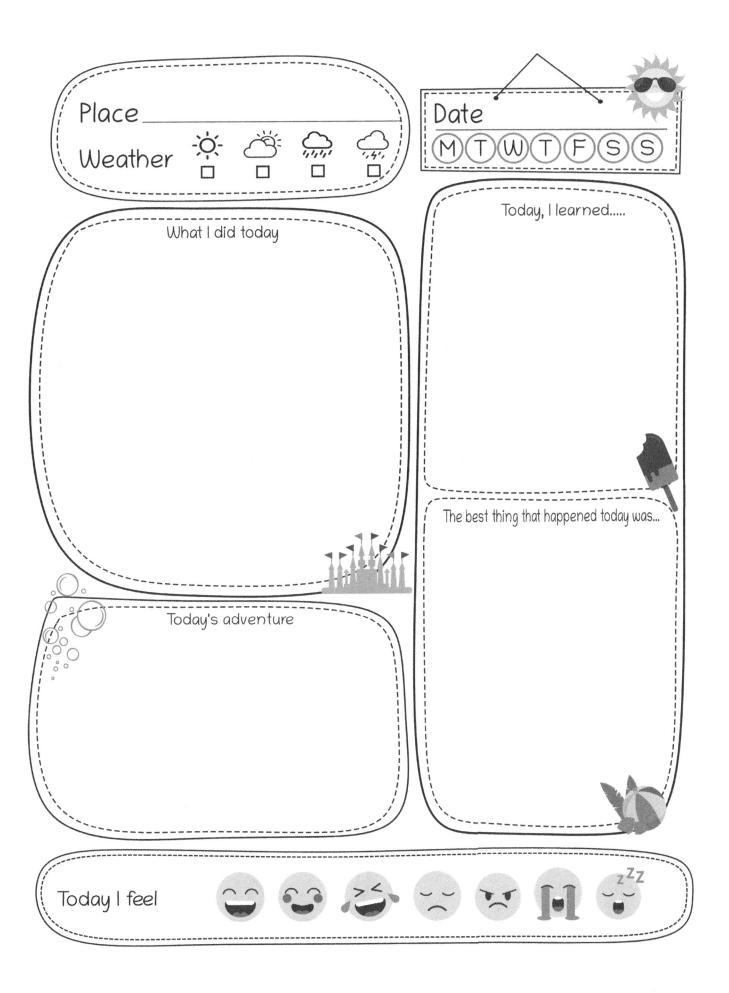

Place _____

Weather ☀ ☁ ☔ ☁
☐ ☐ ☐ ☐

Date _____
Ⓜ Ⓣ Ⓦ Ⓣ Ⓕ Ⓢ Ⓢ

What I did today

Today, I learned.....

The best thing that happened today was...

Today's adventure

Today I feel

My favorite
rainy day
activity is

My favorite
outdoors
summer
activity is

hot!

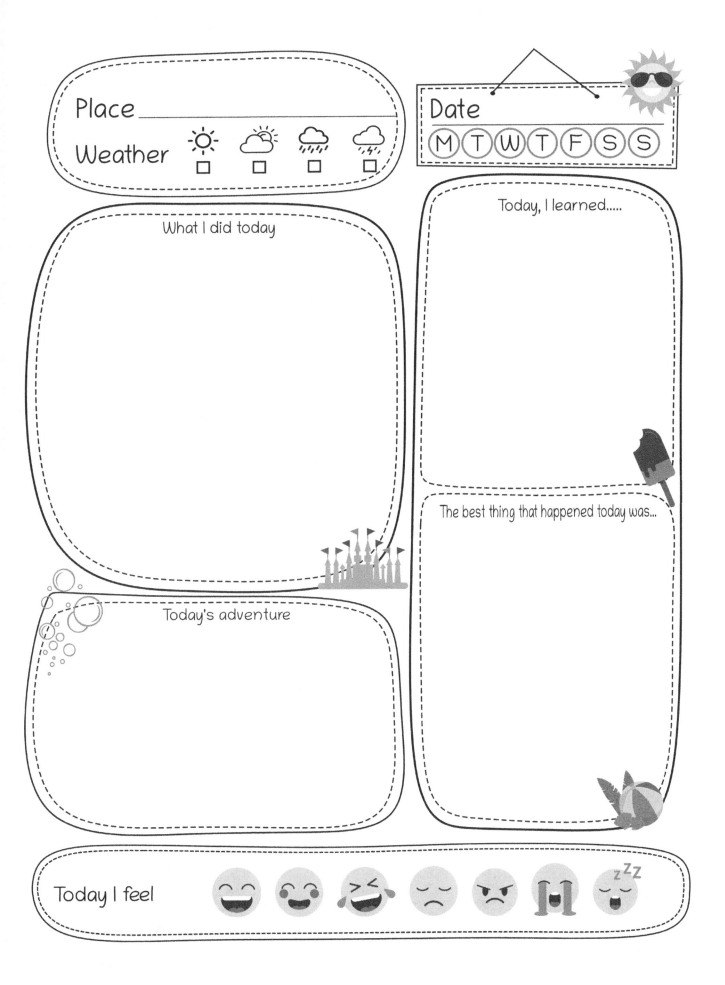

Place _____

Weather ☀ ⛅ 🌧 ⛈

Date _____
Ⓜ Ⓣ Ⓦ Ⓣ Ⓕ Ⓢ Ⓢ

What I did today

Today, I learned.....

The best thing that happened today was...

Today's adventure

Today I feel

Place _____

Weather ☀ ☁ 🌧 ⛈
         ☐ ☐ ☐ ☐

Date _____
Ⓜ Ⓣ Ⓦ Ⓣ Ⓕ Ⓢ Ⓢ

What I did today

Today, I learned......

The best thing that happened today was...

Today's adventure

Today I feel 😄 😊 😆 😔 😠 😭 😴

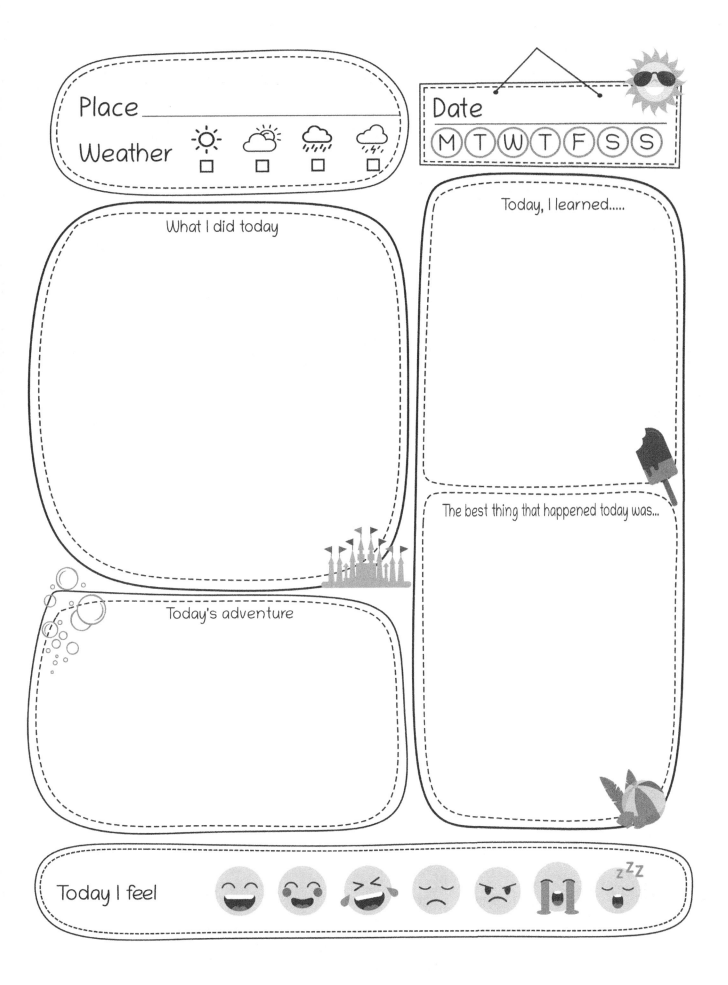

Place _____

Weather ☀ ☁ ⛆ ⛈
        ☐ ☐ ☐ ☐

Date _____
M T W T F S S

What I did today

Today, I learned.....

The best thing that happened today was...

Today's adventure

Today I feel

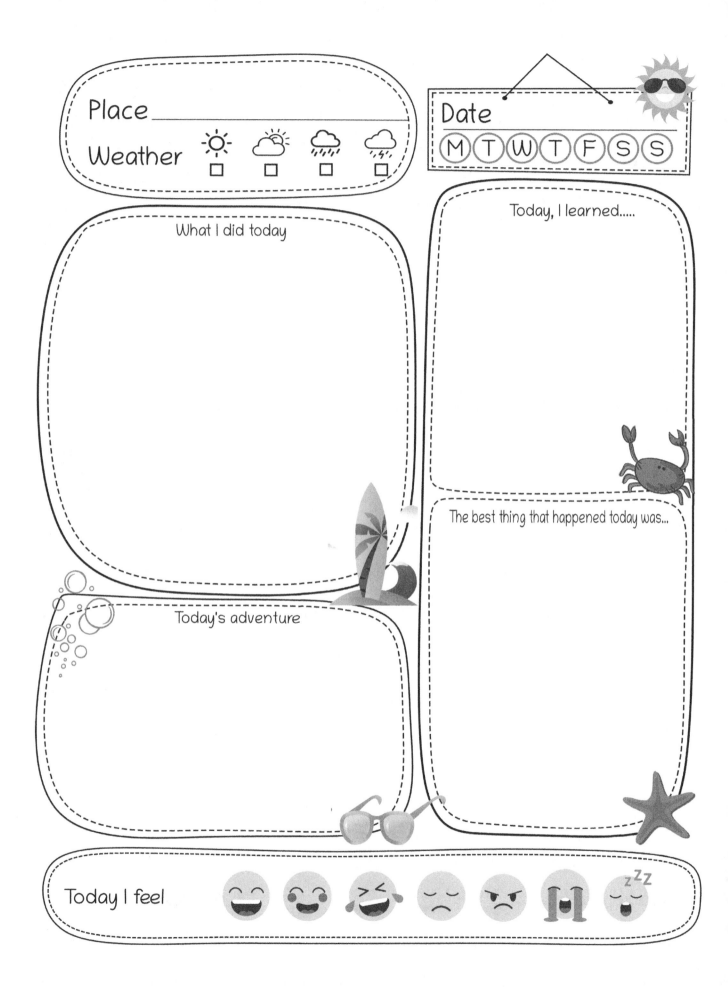

Place _____

Weather ☀ ⛅ 🌧 🌧

Date _____
M T W T F S S

What I did today

Today, I learned.....

Today's adventure

The best thing that happened today was...

Today I feel 😄 😊 😆 😔 😠 😭 😴

My favorite memory from this summer

_____

_____

_____

_____

_____

_____

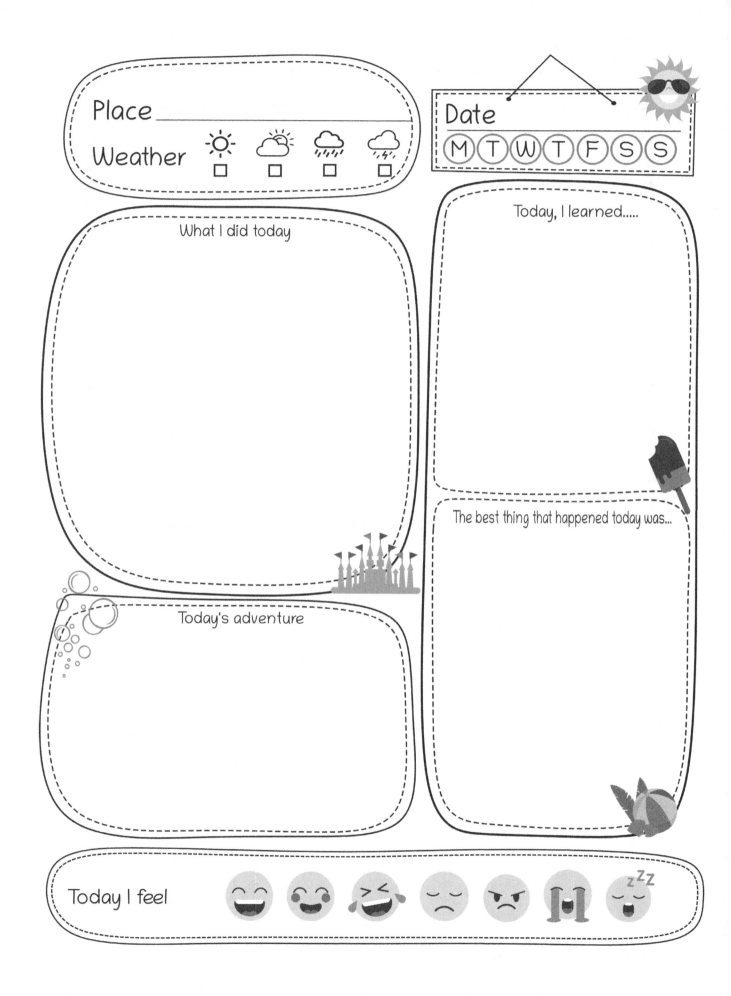

Place _____

Weather ☀ ⛅ 🌧 ⛈

Date _____
M T W T F S S

What I did today

Today, I learned.....

The best thing that happened today was...

Today's adventure

Today I feel

Place _____

Weather ☀ ⛅ 🌧 🌧 ☐ ☐ ☐ ☐

Date _____

M T W T F S S

What I did today

Today, I learned.....

The best thing that happened today was...

Today's adventure

Today I feel

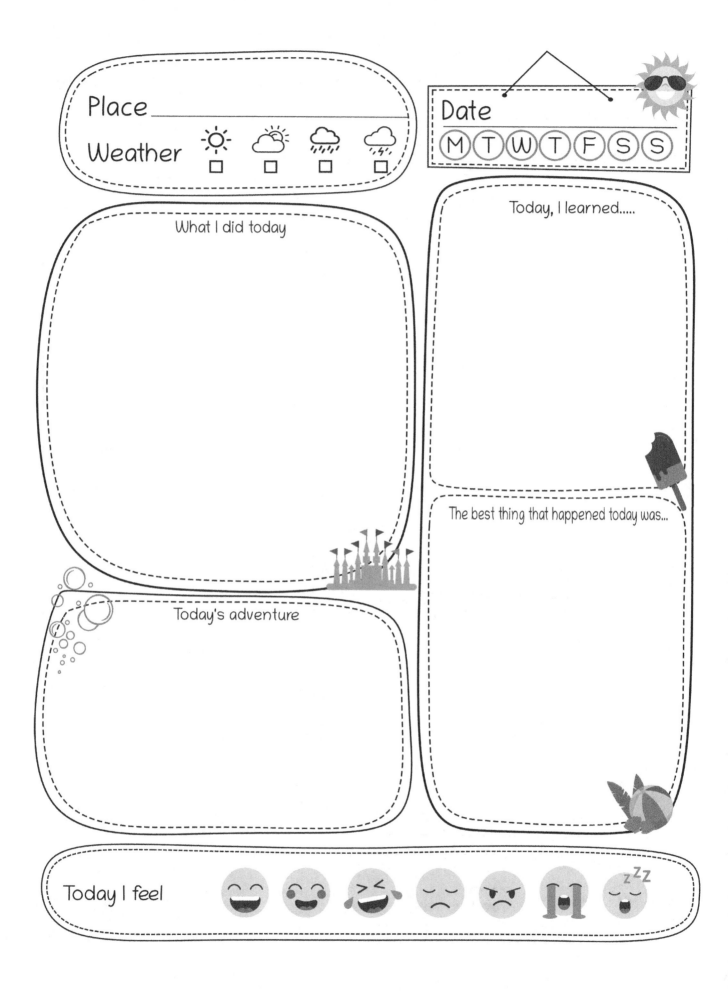

Place _____

Weather ☀ ⛅ 🌧 ⛈

Date _____
M T W T F S S

What I did today

Today, I learned.....

The best thing that happened today was...

Today's adventure

Today I feel

Place _____

Weather ☀ ⛅ 🌧 ⛈
□ □ □ □

Date _____
M T W T F S S

What I did today

Today, I learned.....

The best thing that happened today was...

Today's adventure

Today I feel

The thing I will miss most about summer when the school starts

The thing I am most looking forward to about school

Random thoughts/doodles/pictures.

Random thoughts/doodles/pictures.

Random thoughts/doodles/pictures.

Random thoughts/doodles/pictures.

Made in United States
North Haven, CT
24 June 2022